GETTING STARTED IN FLY FISHING

GETTING STARTED IN

FLY FISHING

TOM FULLER

RAGGED MOUNTAIN PRESS / McGRAW-HILL

Camden, Maine • New York • Chicago • San Francisco • Lisbon • London •
Madrid • Mexico City • Milan • New Delhi • San Juan • Seoul • Singapore •
Sydney • Toronto

The McGraw·Hill Companies

1 2 3 4 5 6 7 8 9 0 DOC DOC 0 9 8 7 6 5 4

Library of Congress Cataloging-in-Publication Data
Fuller, Tom, 1948–
  Getting started in fly fishing / Tom Fuller.
      p.   cm.
Includes bibliographical references and index.
  ISBN 0-07-142787-2
  1. Fly fishing. I. Title.
  SH456.F845 2004
  799.12'4—dc22   2004003445

Questions regarding the content of this book should be addressed to
Ragged Mountain Press
P.O. Box 220
Camden, ME 04843
www.raggedmountainpress.com

Questions regarding the ordering of this book should be addressed to
The McGraw-Hill Companies
Customer Service Department
P.O. Box 547
Blacklick, OH 43004
Retail customers: 1-800-262-4729
Bookstores: 1-800-722-4726

Photographs by Pat and Tom Fuller unless otherwise noted.
Many thanks to The Orvis Company and Cabela's for photos. Thanks also to Paul McGurren at Maine Sport, and to Jim Dugan Photography.
Illustrations by Whitney Martin unless otherwise noted.

For Pat, again and always.

Contents

Acknowledgments

Books like this usually originate with an author's perception that there is a need for a new one, but that was not the case here. When Jonathan Eaton, the editorial director at International Marine / Ragged Mountain Press, approached me to do an introductory book about fly fishing, I promptly argued that it was quite unnecessary because there were so many titles already out there.

Yet Jonathan had surveyed the literature (had, in essence, done my job) and had found that most introductory books were top-heavy in expansive detail and very short on accomplishing the task at hand, namely getting people on the water and catching fish with a fly rod as soon as possible. He wanted a book that worked for the readers.

After my initial reluctance, and after I, too, had surveyed the introductory books that were available, the two of us developed the concept of this book. We came from opposite ends of fly fishing. Jonathan had very limited experience with fly fishing, and I have been consumed with it for forty years. It was his clear eye as a newcomer to the sport that provided the overriding focus of this book—to quickly get people casting competently and catching fish on a fly with as little extraneous information as possible. And it was his idea to build upon the early experiences of new fly fishers with further information, but farther along in the book. I think it has worked exceptionally well. Thanks, Jon.

I combined the opportunity that Jon presented to me with my experiences in teaching fly fishing at the behest of Ellie Horwitz, Information and Education Chief of the Massachusetts Division of Fisheries and Wildlife. Ellie organizes the Becoming an Outdoorswoman (BOW) events for the Division, and some years ago she asked if I would help teach the fly fishing section. Again I was reluctant. I'm a writer, not a teacher. But I started teaching under the competent wing of Jim Lafley, who had put together an excellent five-page handout about fly fishing, and under the watchful eye of my wife Pat, a veteran teacher herself.

If it was Ellie, Jim, and Pat who gave me the opportunity to teach fly fishing, it was the many women students who quickly let me know when I was off track. My digressions were quickly stifled as these wonderful and enthusiastic people let me know they had limited time, they wanted to learn how to put a fly fishing outfit together, they wanted to know the basics of casting, and then they wanted to catch fish—and all in the space of one day. Together, we've been doing just that for several years now, and their input has been invaluable to this book.

During the actual writing of a book of this kind, I quickly realized that I needed a unique individual who is an accomplished writer and an accomplished fly fisher. Spence Conley is both, and he willingly spent uncounted hours reading the manuscript, commenting on it, and making valued comments about my writing and about my perceptions of many aspects of fly fishing. Thanks also to David Conti for his thoughtful review of the manuscript and his valuable suggestions.

It was also valuable to have new fly fishers scan the manuscript for confusing or poorly written passages. Bill and Judy Wells are not only good friends, they willingly pointed out areas that needed work. And Cheryl McNamee agreed to take on the reading task as someone who had never touched a fly rod. Her input made me write and rewrite from the perspective of someone absolutely new to the sport. A big thanks to all of you.

The person that I most closely worked with was my wife Pat. She read every word of every draft of this book. Her critical reading and unbiased eye made the book better in all areas.

Introduction

If you've picked up this book, you have at least some curiosity about fly fishing. It might be a simple admiration for the way a fly line artfully arcs out first behind and then in front of an experienced fly fisher. It might be the knowledge that fly casters always seem to catch more fish. Or it might be that the fly fishers you've encountered unconsciously convey the impression that there's a mystique to the brotherhood (or sisterhood) of the fly. Yet before you can pinpoint why fly fishing has attracted you, you need some knowledge of what fly fishing is all about. You need to know the fundamentals.

The first three chapters of this book, therefore, cover the basics of a minimal fly fishing outfit, tying on an effective fly, casting it to where a fish should be hiding, and hooking and landing your first fish. With just the barest luck you can acquire all these fundamental skills and catch your first fish on your first outing. I know this because I've seen it happen over and over again through my many years of teaching fly fishing. That first day will also get you past the biggest hurdle of fly fishing—namely, realizing that the cast itself is an easy skill to acquire.

With these basic skills mastered, you can approach nearly any species of fish, from pumpkinseeds to stripers, and any water—fresh or salt, flowing or still—knowing that you can get a fly in front of a fish, expect the fish to take the fly, and land the fish effectively. Yet there is much, much more to fly fishing. There are skills, nuances, and knowledge to be gained through instruction and experience that always enhance the craft and make it fascinating for a lifetime.

Chapters 4 and 5 will begin to delve into those aspects of fly fishing that have made it addictive for centuries. Trout have always been the preferred quarry of fly fishers, and for good reason. Although any fish that swims in fresh or salt water is fair game for the fly-rodder (and we'll look into other species later in the book), trout started it all by being so desirable to catch and by feeding mainly on aquatic insects.

From the very first time an angler sought to catch trout with imitations of insects up to this day, two indisputable facts remain: the insects themselves are too fragile and tiny to thread onto hooks, and their imitations, made of airy feathers and fur, are too light to cast the same way we cast baits or lures. Thus "fly" fishing. Add to this that trout live in the most beautiful regions on earth in cold-water streams, rivers, lakes, and ponds, and that each of these waters offers a never-repeated variety of scenery, habitat, and opportunities, and you begin to understand the allure of fly fishing. Yes, fly casting can be learned in a day and often in a half hour, but learning all there is to know about catching trout with a fly is a lifelong passion. You can never know it all, but each thing you learn immerses you more deeply in the mysteries of fly fishing.

So chapters 4 and 5 deal with beginning to see the water, with starting to understand where the fish should be holding, and with choosing an artificial fly and a method of presenting it that respond appropriately to what you've observed.

Part 2 of the book builds on the lessons of part 1. With a couple of days of angling under your belt, you'll inevitably begin to meet challenges that can be baffling, especially when the basic cast needs to become a bit more complex. As you try to meet these challenges, certain problems arise, and chapter 6 addresses them. The remaining four chapters of part 2 continue to expand upon the lore of identifying the insects trout feed on, choosing and presenting artificial flies accordingly, knowing where they live, and developing a steward's care for the fragile and limited habitat we call "trout water."

If I've done my job in the first two parts of this book, and if you do yours by getting out on the water as soon and as often as possible, then by the time you're ready for part 3 you'll know that fly fishing is an activity you want to pursue in depth, and quite likely for life. I merely scratch the surface of that depth in part 3. In chapter 11, we open a window on salmon and steelhead fishing and see that great fly fishing is available for innumerable fresh- and saltwater fish.

Finally, chapter 12 discusses artificial flies. For more than eight hundred years, fly fishers have been documenting the particulars of the flies they've created. (They've been using flies much longer than that!) And over the hundreds of years since, the simple act of applying feathers and fur to fishing hooks has left us with a dizzying array of artificials from which to choose. Chapter 12 brings some order to the confusing field of imitative flies and gives a brief look into how they are tied.

You can pursue your passion for fly fishing to any extent you choose. I know several superb fly fishers who rely on barely a half dozen patterns of flies (and one who uses only one dry fly pattern!), and each of them rarely fishes more than one or two streams near their homes. Some lifelong anglers are expert in many waters and can identify and imitate many varieties of insects throughout the year. And still others revel in traveling throughout North America and the world to fish new streams.

Some fly fishers love both the timeless simplicity of the sport *and* the complexity of its evolution and history, hungrily reading new theories or collecting vintage rods, reels, specialized flies, and art. Others become impassioned about the trout's natural world, identifying hundreds and thousands of insect genera and species, collecting them on the stream, and tying hundreds of fly patterns to imitate subtle nuances of an insect's life cycle and physiology. But most of us don't reach these extremes. Most of us are happy that we know enough about fly fishing to catch a few fish and, above all, to enjoy the experience.

In other words, fly fishing is whatever you make it. It's certainly a superbly efficient method of catching fish, but it can be much more, and each fly fisher will ultimately discover the level of interest that suits him or her.

I hope this book not only gets you started in fly fishing but also gives you a glimpse of what fly fishing can become. Hopefully, the skills you acquire and the interests you develop will become treasured companions for the rest of your life, just as they have for me.

PART ONE

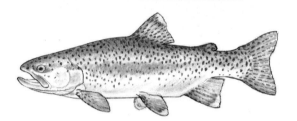

GETTING
OUT THERE

1 The Start-Up Kit

The tools of fly fishing are like the first set of carpentry tools you ever owned. You start with the basics: a saw, a hammer, and a measuring tape; a rod, a reel, and a few flies. These few tools will serve you well as you learn the craft. With experience, however, you may want a more precise saw (maybe a compound miter saw) or a fly rod for specialized circumstances (say Atlantic salmon fishing). You may want a light hammer for finish work or a fly tying kit to make your own flies. And yet, if you choose your first tools wisely, you'll find yourself coming back to them time and again regardless of how expansive your collection gets.

ROD, REEL, AND LINE

A fly rod and reel outfit looks and feels different from all other types of fishing tackle because the rod puts its fishing lure—the fly—onto and into the water in a unique way. Manipulating, or casting, the fly line itself, rather than a heavy lure, sends the air-light artificial fly at its end sailing over the water to land where you want it. That's why you see a gracefully arcing line both behind and in front of a fly caster. With a fly rod, you're casting the line itself, not some heavy weight at its end.

One consequence is that the fly reel is unimportant in casting, so it's always mounted at the butt of the rod—the thick lower end—below the grip for your casting hand and thus out of the way.

Fly rods are usually 8 to 9 feet long and have many small eyelets along their length. The *eyelets*, also called line guides, hold the line close to the rod. The forward and backward action that you give to the rod is how you control and manipulate the line— how you make the cast. You can quickly identify a fly rod, as opposed to a surf-casting or spinning rod, because the fly rod will be thin and long, will have a reel seat at its butt end, and will have numerous small line guides along its length.

Because you're casting the line, not the fly, it's necessarily thicker than any other fishing line you've seen. It has weight, although not much, and this weight is desig-

Parts of a fly rod

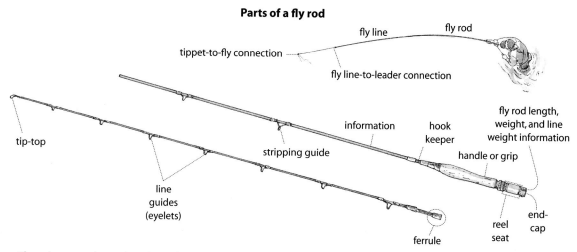

Fly rod nomenclature is universal, and knowing it will help you understand exactly how a rod is put together. For instance, the *ferrule* is where the two parts of the rod in the illustration are joined, but rods can have more than one ferrule, and up to a dozen. A three-ferrule rod has three component pieces, a four-ferrule rod has four, and so on, and the tip-top line guide is always on the end of the last piece of the rod. Likewise, line guides, or eyelets, can be round guides, like the stripping guide, or snake guides, which are strong pieces of wire that don't connect except with the rod, but they're always line guides. *(Elayne Sears)*

nated as a number, generally 3 through 8—the lower the number, the lighter the line. There are specialty lines that are lighter, 1s and 2s, and heavier, 9s through 14s.

Fly rods are designed to cast certain weights of fly line: a 3-weight fly rod requires a 3-weight line, and this designation should be printed right on the rod, near the grip or on the metal endcap. Often a fly rod's length (say 8 feet), actual weight (say 3½ ounces), and compatible line weight (in this case 6-weight) are printed together on the rod—for example, "8'–3½ oz.–6."

Over the years, fly rods have been made from split bamboo, tubular steel, greenheart wood, fiberglass, boron, and graphite fibers, to name a few materials. Nowadays they are made almost exclusively from graphite, because this material is light, strong, and long lasting, or split bamboo, the traditional material that brought cane rods and fly fishing to the masses. Graphite rod prices vary from inexpensive to pricey, while modern cane rods are always expensive.

The high degree of sophistication now used in manipulating the graphite fibers when making fly rods confers to each rod an important design feature known as its *action* or *flex.* Simply put, this refers to the bend the rod takes as it casts the line. Generally, rods come in fast action or flex tips, medium action or mid-flex, and slow action or full-flex. Action, or flex, can become important as you become more experi-

MATCHING FISH TO ROD AND LINE WEIGHT

Species and Context	Rod and Line Weight Range
Small Trout and Panfish	1–3 weight
Trout	
Small Stream	1–3 weight
Midsized Streams and Rivers	3–6 weight
Wide Rivers, Lakes	4–7 weight
Smallmouth Bass	5–9 weight
Largemouth Bass	5–9 weight
Northern Pike and Muskie	7–10 weight
Steelhead and Light Salmon	6–9 weight
Heavy Salmon, Atlantic and Pacific	8–10 weight
Bonefish	6–9 weight
Permit	9–11 weight
Bluefish, Striped Bass	8–10 weight
False Albacore and Bonito	8–10 weight
Redfish, Snook, and Sea Trout	7–10 weight
Tarpon	9–12 weight
Billfish and Other Large Pelagic Species	12–14 weight

LEFT: Rod and line weight indicate the heft and strength of the outfit. Lighter rods and lines are for lighter fish or when delicate presentations are needed to entice wary fish. Bear in mind that this thumbnail guide to choosing the weight of your outfit is not chiseled in stone. A 5-weight outfit, when matched with a proper reel and experienced angler, can certainly catch striped bass, salmon, and big pike.

Split bamboo (cane) fly rods brought fly fishing to the masses when automation methods were applied to produce them. These days, however, mass-produced cane rods have been largely replaced by graphite rods *(shown here)*, which add a consistency not always present in bamboo. Nevertheless, fine, handmade cane rods are still produced and valued. *(Cheyenne Rouse Photography)*

enced, but even long-time anglers say that a medium-action, mid-flex rod covers the widest variety of situations.

Because the fly line is so critical to the cast, a number of designs are available. *Level* lines, which have their weight equally distributed along their entire length (about 90 feet, but up to 105 feet long), are designated with an L on their packaging. They are few and far between. *Weight-forward* lines (WF) put more weight toward the business end of the line to encourage longer casts. *Double-tapered* lines (DT) have a taper

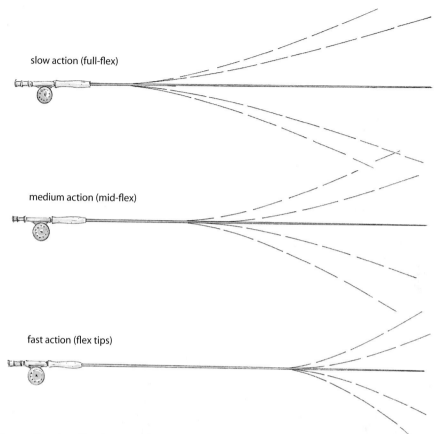

slow action (full-flex)

medium action (mid-flex)

fast action (flex tips)

Fly rod action, or flex, describes how much and where the rod bends when it's loaded by the backcast and forecast. A fast-action rod flexes very little, allowing an angler to cast with tighter loops. This adds distance but requires excellent technique. A slow-action rod flexes the most, restricting distance but increasing the "feel" of the rod, which makes it easier to detect strikes on underwater flies, especially wet flies and nymphs. *(Elayne Sears)*

at both ends so that you can flip them end for end if they become worn, which rarely happens nowadays. Some lines are designed to make exceptionally long casts; designated *shooting-head* lines (SH), these are short (30-foot) lengths of fly line attached to a thin running line and are specialty items requiring unique tactics.

In addition, some fly lines float, some sink, and some have just a portion at the end that sinks, the designations being F, S, or ST (sinking tip), respectively. So when you're choosing lines, you'll probably see something like "WF-6-F," which translates into a "weight-forward, 6-weight, floating line." Line design is a favorite area of improvement, with new coatings and cores appearing yearly, but all lines can be understood with these few designations.

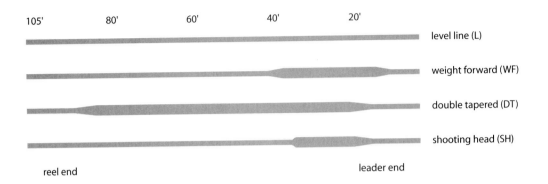

105'	80'	60'	40'	20'	
					level line (L)
					weight forward (WF)
					double tapered (DT)
					shooting head (SH)

reel end   leader end

Fly line tapers describe the shape of the fly line in profile. For fishing, weight-forward and double-tapered lines are most common, with the former adding to the length of line that can be cast and the latter enhancing the "feel" of what's happening to the fly, especially underwater. A shooting-head line, with about 30 feet of fly line attached to a long length of thin running line, is used strictly for exceptionally long casts.

Putting this information about rods and lines together, we see that for trout you'll probably want a 5- or 6-weight outfit and a rod that is 8 to 9 feet long with a medium action. Your most versatile line will be a WF-6-F.

Fly reels consist of a frame, the drag system, and a spool. The frame is the superstructure that attaches to the rod, contains the drag system, and holds the spool. Reels make no contribution to the cast—indeed, they are just line holders—but the drag system becomes important when you've hooked a fish, especially a big fish.

Virtually every reel now comes with a built-in drag system with which to adjust the tension of the line as it comes off the reel. Increase this tension and a fish must work harder to pull off more line; decrease it and the line comes off more easily. It's important to adjust the drag depending on how much weight is required to break the line that attaches the fly to the fly line (see Leader and Tippet below).

Fly reels have nothing to do with casting the fly line, but they're versatile tools just the same. Their spools of line can be changed easily, and their good drag systems are valuable when battling large fish. *(Cabela's)*

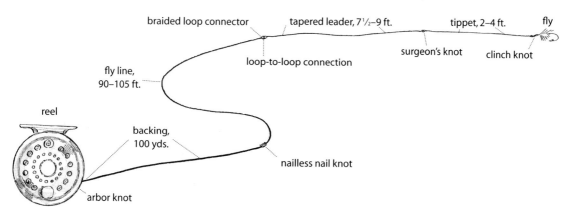

Backing, fly line, leader, and tippet. See chapter 2 for knots. *(Elayne Sears)*

On most reels the spools of line can be removed and replaced. This becomes important when you want to carry different types of line—say a floating line for dry flies, a sinking-tip line to fish nymphs, and a full sinking line to get down deep in lakes or ponds. Instead of carrying (and buying) three different reels, you just buy different spools for the same reel.

If you buy a ready-to-use outfit, you'll notice that the fly line wound onto the reel fills the reel almost to the rim. This is because a much thinner line has been wound onto the reel first. It's known as *backing* and has two functions. First, it lays a foundation on the spool so that the fly line itself, when tied to the backing and wound on top of it, almost completely fills the spool. This allows you to gain as much line as possible with each turn when you crank the line back onto the reel while playing a fish. Second, when a big fish pulls all your fly line off the reel, you still have the backing, usually 300 feet or more, to keep you attached to the fish. (For attaching backing, see Knots, in chapter 2.)

These outfits—fly rod, reel, and line—*can* be expensive, but they don't *have* to be. To start, either borrow one from a friend or buy an inexpensive outfit from a fly fishing shop, a mail-order company, or a local discount store. You can get an adequate outfit for under $100, or for about $300 you can get a very nice outfit to learn on and then to fish with for years to come.

LEADER AND TIPPET

As I've said, fly lines are relatively thick for casting. But the flies we're trying to get in front of fish are small and light, often extremely so. These flies literally cannot be threaded onto a fly line, and even if they could be, the thick line, visible at close range to fish, would appear unnatural and would scare them away. So we need something between the fly line and the fly that's both relatively invisible and thin enough to tie the fly onto—a *leader*.

Leaders are usually lengths of solid monofilament line from 7½ feet to 12 feet or more long. Some are made of several pieces of thin monofilament braided together. Attached to the end of the fly line (see Knots, in chapter 2) they provide that critical link between fly line and fly. While leaders *can* be simple, uniform lengths of the same monofilament line used on spinning reels, for our purposes—namely, trout fishing—the leaders need to *taper* from a thick end tied to the fly line to the much thinner end to which the fly is tied in an effort to fool the trout.

These tapered leaders will keep unrolling, just as the fly line does, at the end of the cast. In a good cast, the fly ends up right out at the end of the forward-extended invisible leader. If the leader weren't tapered, the very light monofilament needed to present a small fly

The connection between the fly line and the fly is called a leader and is almost always tapered from a heavy butt section to a lighter tippet. Leaders can be made from a single strand of monofilament, from knotted sections of decreasing diameter monofilament, or from many small-diameter lengths of monofilament braided together. Spools of tippet material are used to replace the end of the leader—the tippet—when it becomes too short from changing or losing flies. *(Cabela's)*

wouldn't unroll but would end up in a pile of line coiled around the fly, the sight of which would cause the fish to flee.

The end of the leader where the fly attaches is known as the *tippet*, and now we're out where the action is. Tippets are critical, and understanding what they do is our first step toward becoming efficient fly *fishers*, and not just good fly *casters*.

When you pick up a package that contains a tapered leader, you'll notice two prominent numbers. The first is easy to understand. It's the length of the leader. The second is a bit more obscure. It reveals the diameter of the tapered leader at its action end, where you'll attach the fly. This diameter is given in "X" sizes, ranging from 0X to 8X (sometimes 9X or 10X). The higher the number, the *smaller* the diameter, and we're talking really thin line when we get out past 7X. In fact, a 7X tippet is something like 0.004 inch in diameter, while a 3X tippet is twice that thick, 0.008 inch.

The thickness of the tippet matters for two reasons. First, as the thickness increases, so, logically, does its strength. 3X tippets are rated to break at 8½ to 9 pounds, while 7X tippets are rated at 2½ pounds. Yet we want to use as thin a tippet as possible because we want it to be as invisible as possible. Yes, fish are that fussy. Their lives depend on it. The relative strength of the tippet is also critical when you're setting the drag on your reel.

Second, and as important, the thickness of your tippet helps determine how large a fly you can tie onto it and still have the fly land at the end of the tippet and not in a puddle of line. Even though we think of flies as nearly weightless, they aren't. Larger flies are heavier, and because we're dealing with such fine diameters in tippets, the weight of the fly we're casting is significant. Larger-diameter tippets propel large flies

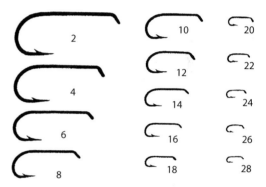

Artificial flies may be exceptionally light, but they do have weight. Tippet size, which is just a short-hand designation for the diameter and strength of the tippet, must match fly size to ensure that the weight of the fly doesn't drop it to the water before the fly line, leader, and tippet are fully extended. The life-sized hook chart shows just how much larger a size 2 hook is than a size 28.

Mustad Hooks 94840, standard dry fly hooks (actual size)

Tippet Size	Diameter	Strength (lb. test)	Fly Hook Sizes
0X	0.011	15.5	1/0, 2, 4
1X	0.010	13.5	2, 4, 6
2X	0.009	11.5	6, 8, 10
3X	0.008	8.5	10, 12, 14
4X	0.007	6.0	12, 14, 16
5X	0.006	4.5	14, 16, 18
6X	0.005	3.5	16, 18, 20, 22
7X	0.004	2.5	18, 20, 22, 24
8X	0.003	1.5	22, 24, 26, 28

out to their very end, but we can use thinner tippets for smaller flies.

Hook sizes follow the same rule; the higher the number, the *smaller* the hook. Unfortunately, they don't coincide with tippet size. You don't use a size 7 hook on a 7X tippet. But you do use a thinner tippet with smaller hooks. (See table previous page.)

Because most trout flies are in the range of hook sizes 10 to 18, you'll only need leaders with tippets ranging from 3X to 5X, or three leaders tapering to 3X, 4X, and 5X. Buy them with loops at both ends (see Knots, in chapter 2). Later in your angling career, as you broaden the types and sizes of artificial flies you use, you may want tippets both larger and smaller than these.

As you fish more and more, you'll find that the tippet on the end of your leader quickly gets shorter. You'll certainly change flies often, and you'll clip off a little bit of tippet each time. And if you're like me, too many flies will end up in the bushes, and breaking them off leaves even more tippet material behind. Changing an entire leader each time the tippet gets too short is expensive, so buy some spools of tippet material. They're sold using the same "X" formula. Then when the leader gets too short, just tie on some new tippet material (see Knots, in chapter 2).

There are wide variations among rods, reels, lines, and leaders, variations that may become important when you target fish like striped bass or Atlantic salmon, tarpon or largemouth bass, sharks or pumpkinseeds. The outfit that we've designed here comprises good middle ground for an average-sized fish like trout. Downsize it, say to a 3- or 4-weight outfit, if you'll be fishing small waters, such as brush-choked or small mountain streams, for smaller fish. Upsize it as your water and fish get larger.

FLIES

Along with fly fishing tackle for nearly any species of fish that swims in fresh water or salt, there are also artificial flies for nearly any fish you might want to target. Sailfish, pompano, northern pike, or even carp, it doesn't matter. There are flies to catch each one.

At the risk of seeming a myopic purist, however, I'll focus here on trout flies. Trout (and I'm talking here about *all* trout species) have always been a desirable fish to catch. They fight hard, they jump, and they taste good. They're a manageable size, not too little or too big. And much of their feeding activity focuses on aquatic insects that we can see sitting in or near the water and that we can imitate in both their air-breathing and their underwater phases. In addition, trout anglers over the last hundred years have been expanding the breadth of the imitations they use to include just about anything a trout will consume. Learn the skills of observation and imitation of what trout eat, and you can apply those skills to most other species. It rarely works the other way around.

Trout flies come in a splendid variety of sizes and types, but in general they can be classified as dry flies, nymphs, wet flies, and streamers. *Dry flies* float on top of the surface film of water and are visible to the angler, while the other three types are fished below the surface. *Nymphs* imitate aquatic insects before they metamorphose from water-breathing organisms to their air-breathing mature forms. *Wet flies* can also imitate these water-breathing stages, or they can be simple curiosities that attract fish with their flash and action. And *streamers*, in general, imitate small feed fish, although they can be attractors, too. The next chapter describes how each of these types of flies should look to the fish and how they should be presented.

For now, we need to know which basic fly patterns to acquire, and the best way to do this is to talk to an angler who frequents a nearby water or to go into a local fly shop and ask. The shop owner, especially, should be helpful. He's in the business of selling flies, but he also knows that he needs to suggest fly patterns that will work on a particular piece of water at a particular time of year. If he wanders away from this philosophy, he'll soon find his customers going elsewhere. If he's been in business for a few years, you should be able to trust his advice.

If getting up-to-date local advice isn't possible, start with a generic, all-purpose dry fly such as an Adams or a Royal Wulff and obtain a half dozen of each in two or three sizes. As you get started in fly fishing, dry flies will help you hone both your casting and your stream-craft skills. (For more on stream craft, see chapter 4.) This is because they're the only type of fly you can see. You'll be able to see if the fly stretches all the way out to the end of your line and leader when you cast it, and you'll be able to see how the flow of a stream affects the fly on the end of your line.

As you become confident in your skills and begin to focus more closely on actually catching fish, you'll expand your collection of flies. Choosing which flies to use in any of a seemingly infinite variety of situations is one of those lifelong fascinations for many fly fishers. Observation, conversation, expert professional and amateur advice, and plain curiosity will all come into play in deciding which flies to carry. Making your choices becomes a very personal thing. Yet acquiring flies can also follow some simple personal rules, like when and where you fish and what you fish for. Chap-

Two patterns of dry flies in two or three sizes will begin your collection of flies nicely—the Royal Wulff *(left)* and the Adams *(right).* Choose dry flies to start because you will be able to see how the current affects them as they drift along a stream. These flies will catch plenty of trout. *(Orvis)*

ters 4 and 5 and sections of parts 2 and 3 deal with fly selection in more detail. For now, get some Adams and Royal Wulff dry flies.

TOOLS: FLY BOXES, NIPPERS, HEMOSTATS, FLY FLOATANT, LANDING NET, AND SUNSCREEN

Manufacturers are always trying to come up with the next widget for fly fishers. In any fly fishing catalog or store, you can quickly become overwhelmed with the array of widgets artfully displayed to tempt you. For my money (and I've earned some renown for Yankee thrift), the following items are, if not essential, then at least very helpful.

BARBED VERSUS BARBLESS HOOKS

Artificial flies can be tied on hooks that either do or do not have barbs. The argument for a barb is that it makes it more difficult for the fish to throw the fly. Some authorities also believe a barb prevents a hook from penetrating a fish's flesh too deeply. Others argue that barb-less hooks don't make as big a wound in a fish's mouth and make releasing a fish easier. The choice is yours. Certain waters require barbless hooks, or at least hooks with the barbs pinched down. Your hemostats (see photo oposite, and page 18) work well in pinching down barbs.

Fly boxes carry your flies, and then you carry the boxes instead of individual flies. How many fly boxes you carry is directly proportional to how enamored you become of different types and patterns of flies, but here are some guidelines. Fly boxes should be large enough to carry several dozen flies but small enough to put into a shirt or vest pocket. They should hold the flies so that you can see them individually. You'll be looking for particular flies when you're on the stream, and if all your flies are stuffed into Altoid tins, you'll probably spill a few flies when you're pawing through them looking for the one you want.

I like fly boxes with foam interiors I can stick the points of the hooks into. The flies stay organized and stay in the box when you drop it into the water, which you'll do at least once a

Although you may start with a limited collection of flies, the longer you fish, the more flies you'll acquire. The variety of insects you encounter and want to imitate, the situations and species of fish you may face, and the fly fisher's eternal need to acquire "just a few more flies" all conspire to grow your collection. (Cabela's)

year and probably once a trip. Many fly boxes are now built to float, again so that when you inevitably drop one, it won't sink to the bottom of the stream or lake. I like that. And some people, like me, are clumsy enough to appreciate a little eyelet on the outside corner of the box so it can be tied with a piece of string to a belt loop or vest. I once watched a floating fly box that contained some of my most prized flies fall into the West Branch of the Penobscot River in Maine, a famously fast-flowing river, and before I could blink twice that box was enjoying an Atlantic Ocean cruise.

Nippers are nail clipper–like tools with which you can snip the extra tippet material close to the knot that holds the fly. You'll also need to clip off lengths of tippet material from the spool and to clip off flies when you're done fishing. You can use actual nail clippers, but manufacturers are producing little specialized, flat-bladed nippers, most of which have a sharp needle built into the opposite end that helps you untangle leader snarls and clear the eyes of flies that might be clogged with head cement or old tippet material. Another helpful widget is a *zinger*, a retractable length of cord

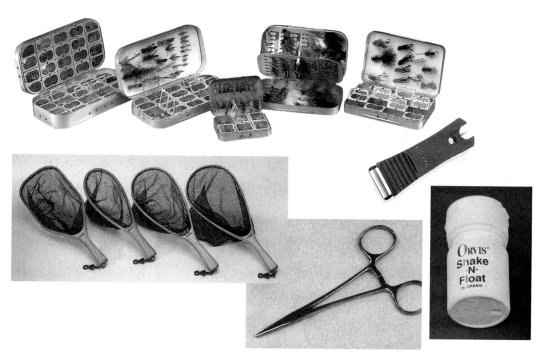

Your initial collection of accessories should include *(clockwise from top)* fly boxes, nippers, fly floatant, hemostats, a landing net, and sunscreen *(not shown)*. As you fly fish more and more, you may find yourself acquiring other widgets, like a stream thermometer, a small seining net, nontoxic split shot, indicator yarn or putty, extra leaders and spools of tippet material, sunglasses, magnifying glasses, other pastes for sinking flies or floating leaders, and more. Your vest will need plenty of roomy pockets! *(Cabela's, Orvis, Gil Alfring)*

that you pin to your shirt or vest with a clip on the end. Put the nippers on the zinger, and the nippers will always be nearby.

Hemostats are surgical tools, like needle-nose pliers, that click closed and stay that way until you release them. Their narrow noses are ideal for extracting hooks from fish, especially when the hooks are too deep in a fish's mouth to reach with fingers. Hemostats are also handy for holding flies, especially small ones, when you're tying them onto your tippet. Just lock the fly into the jaws of the hemostats, and you've got something your hand can hold. (There's another widget designed to do only that— hold flies—but hemostats work almost as well.) Put your hemostats (you only need one, despite the plural noun form) on another zinger and pin them to the other side of your shirt or vest.

There are several types of fly floatant, and now they've become more environmentally friendly. Until recently, fly floatant was a concoction of strange chemicals that helped you keep your dry flies floating simply by dipping them into the solution, then shaking them off. When you shook them off, however, a strange chemical sheen floated downstream. Now you can either apply a gel coating that makes the fly float like a cork, or you can keep a small bottle of beads or crystals that will dry your fly after it has become too wet to float. They're inexpensive enough for you to carry both.

Landing nets are far from essential, and there's a continuing debate whether scooping up a fish that's not entirely played out in a landing net is a better way of releasing it, or if simply running your hand down your tippet to unhook the fish when it *is* played out is better. Manufacturers are now building netting material that's kinder to the scales and protective slime of a fish. They're made mostly of cotton or nylon mesh but also of stretchy rubberized mesh that minimizes the chafing. In no case should you use a landing net made of heavy, knotted monofilament mesh if you intend to release the fish. The knots cut into the slime and scales and can damage a fish's eyes. Larger zingers or magnetic releases hold the net on the back of your vest or shirt for easy access.

Sunscreen is listed here because nothing is as painful as a scalding sunburn on your ears, the back of your neck, or your hands. And if you've ever been sunburned at the beach from a single afternoon of revelry, imagine fishing in the bright sun for a week.

WADERS

Hip boots, waist-high waders, and chest waders keep you dry when you're in the water. If this sounds relatively mundane, remember that some of the very best fly fishing is in the spring and fall when stream and lake water temperatures can range from 40 to 70°F. The optimum water temperature for trout, when they're at their hungriest and

Hip boots, waist-high waders, and chest-high waders come in a variety of grades and prices, from inexpensive to pricey. If you use them to any extent, you may also want to purchase an inexpensive repair kit, as you'll inevitably snag your waders on a branch or piece of wire and spring a leak. *(Cabela's)*

most active, is somewhere between 55 and 65°F. That's cold water, and if you get wet you'll be shivering in a matter of minutes. So, yes, you need waders or hip boots.

Top-end waders are made of breathable fabric, though some folks still opt for neoprene waders. The neoprene used—heavy and stretchy, though still quite pliable—is intended for cold weather and cold water. Breathable waders block water from the outside yet allow your body moisture to escape—a feature you'll appreciate if you must hike to the streambank on a warm day. Breathables are becoming the wader of choice for all seasons because they're roomy enough to accommodate a warm undergarment, like fleece trousers, in cold weather.

Other waders, including those made of rubber or canvas, are available for less money, and hip boots can be the least expensive of all.

Both waders and hip boots come in two variations—boot foot and stocking foot. Boot-foot versions incorporate foot-gear into the garment itself. With stocking-foot versions, you must wear a separate pair of shoes, called wading shoes. The advantage of the latter is that you lace up the shoe so that it fits snugly, like a walking shoe. This can be important if you're walking some distance to a stream or if your ankles require the support. Some boot-foot waders permit you to lace up the boots for additional support. To prevent slipping on slimy rocks, the soles of the boots are faced with felt, or studded like golf shoes, or covered with lugged rubber like hiking shoes. Opt for the felts, and if you are going to be fishing in very weedy areas—say on seaweed-covered rocks at the ocean—you can buy slip-on chains, like ice creepers, that will cut through the ooze.

You can get a good pair of stocking-foot breathable waders for about $150 (some versions cost more), but you'll need wading shoes, and they can cost another $50 to

$200. The same boot-foot version runs about $200, or you can get a decent pair of rubber hip boots down at the discount store for about $25. The choice is yours.

One word of warning: If you've never stepped into the water wearing wading gear, you might be surprised. The water pressure around your legs will grab you with surprising force, which feels all the more alive because your legs stay dry.

CLOTHING AND SUNGLASSES

If you've ever seen pictures of fly fishers in magazines or advertisements, you'll usually see them wearing bright clothing. That's because the editors and advertisers want the people to stick out. They want your eyes to go right to the subject. And this is just what the fish will do if you're wearing those same bright colors. They'll pick you right out, and so will the mosquitoes and blackflies. The fish will hide, and the bugs will bite you. So try to wear drab clothing. And, of course, dress for the weather, especially if it's hot or cold. Layers work wonders when a raw dawn yields to a warm midday. Doff what you don't need, then put it back on at dusk.

In addition, try to wear a shirt with long sleeves and a collar you can turn up. This gives you protection from the sun and, more important, from errant hooks that will otherwise inevitably stick into your neck or arm. Hats, too, keep the sun off your head and fishhooks out of your scalp.

Safety sunglasses are doubly important. A hook in the hand can be removed, and the hand will heal. A hook in the eye . . . well, you get the picture. Plus, polarized sunglasses eliminate the glare coming off the water. You can see down into the water more easily, and you won't end up with a sun-glare headache at the end of the day. Polarized sunglasses come in several colors, but the most predominant are amber and gray. I like amber because it seems to give me better vision in the low light of early morning and late afternoon. And yes, you can easily get them as prescription sunglasses.

VESTS

Vests, too, are optional, but once you try one you might decide it's essential. Vests are engineering marvels designed to give you as many pockets as possible to hold your gear while keeping your arms and hands free to fish. Your vest is destined to be stuffed, worn in all kinds of weather, dirtied, and largely abused, so don't spend a lot of money on it.

But do get as many pockets as you can. Remember, they will hold fly boxes, extra leaders and tippet material, extra spools of line, nippers, hemostats, fly floatant, landing net, sunscreen, sunglasses, snacks, lunch, at least one bottle of water, raingear, car keys, fishing license, and other personal necessities. Yes, I do carry all of this in my own vest,

A reliable and efficient fly fishing outfit—including rod, reel, line, leader, flies, waders, vest, and accessories—can be put together for under $400. If chosen carefully, it will give you years of excellent service.

including eight different fly boxes. I may look a bit overstuffed, but it's all there, right at my fingertips.

Note: Do not, at all costs, put a cell phone into your vest or anywhere on your person. They aren't yet banned from trout waters, but they should be.

This listing covers the basics, and these items will cover 99 percent of the gear you'll ever need to fly fish. Ever the cheapskate, I believe you can buy decent gear, a functional rod, reel, and line outfit, and a good collection of flies and tools for under $400. You'd probably spend that on a weekend of skiing with your significant other. Certainly you can spend more, but you don't have to.

In return for this modest expenditure plus a small investment of time to learn how to use this gear, you can become a fly fisher and enjoy all the attendant benefits and beauty.

2 Before You Wet Your Line

"The true fisherman approaches the first day of fishing with all the sense of wonder and awe of a child approaching Christmas."

ROBERT TRAVER
TROUT MADNESS, **1960**

You've got the equipment—now it's time to begin using it. There are two immediate skills you need before you can begin catching fish: tying the essential knots and casting the fly line. But if you're going to catch your first fish on your first day, you also need to know how to wade in the water, where to fish, and how to make the fly look like something good to eat to a fish. Much of the rest of the book will deal with these last three items in expanding detail, but our goal right now is to get out there and start fishing.

Knots: Attaching the Leader to the Fly Line, the Tippet to the Leader, and the Fly to the Tippet

First of all, there's some assembly required out at the business end of the fly line. You need to make tight connections between the fly line, the leader, the tippet, and the fly. Many a fish is lost because one of these connections is inadequate.

There are so many fishing knots that whole books have been devoted to them, and fly fishers sometimes engage in heated debates about which knots to use, where to use them, and when. But the truth is that just a few knots will serve you in virtually every fly fishing situation, and one of them isn't really a knot.

The knot that isn't a knot is the loop-to-loop connection of the leader to the fly line (see bottom illustration opposite). Many fly lines come with a braided nylon loop already connected to the end. If your fly line doesn't have this loop, add one. A simple and inexpensive kit is available at your local fly shop. Just follow the directions on the package.

To connect the tapered leader to the fly line, pass the loop on the fly line through the loop at the thick end of the leader, then pass the tippet end of the leader through the

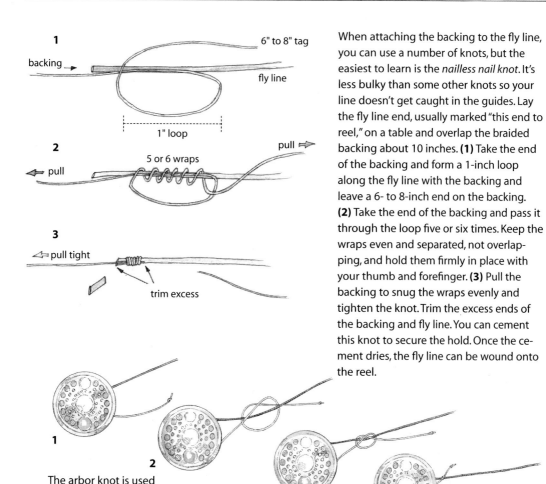

1

backing →

6" to 8" tag

fly line

1" loop

2

5 or 6 wraps

pull ⇨

← pull

3

⇦ pull tight

trim excess

1

2

The arbor knot is used
to tie the backing to the reel. *(Elayne Sears)*

3

4

When attaching the backing to the fly line, you can use a number of knots, but the easiest to learn is the *nailless nail knot*. It's less bulky than some other knots so your line doesn't get caught in the guides. Lay the fly line end, usually marked "this end to reel," on a table and overlap the braided backing about 10 inches. **(1)** Take the end of the backing and form a 1-inch loop along the fly line with the backing and leave a 6- to 8-inch end on the backing. **(2)** Take the end of the backing and pass it through the loop five or six times. Keep the wraps even and separated, not overlapping, and hold them firmly in place with your thumb and forefinger. **(3)** Pull the backing to snug the wraps evenly and tighten the knot. Trim the excess ends of the backing and fly line. You can cement this knot to secure the hold. Once the cement dries, the fly line can be wound onto the reel.

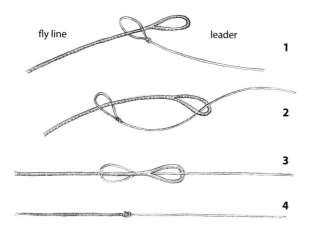

fly line

leader

1

2

3

4

Connecting the fly line to the leader.
(1) Pass the fly line loop through the loop at the thick end of the leader. **(2)** Pass the tippet end of the leader through the fly line loop. **(3–4)** Tighten by pulling in opposite directions. You can disconnect the loops by pushing them toward each other and reversing the process. *(Elayne Sears)*

fly line loop. Pull the tippet and the entire leader through and snug up the connection. All done.

Always be sure to connect loops this way; pass the loop on the thicker line—in this case the fly line—through the loop on the thinner line—here the leader—and then pull the opposite end of the thin line through the loop of the heavier line and tighten. This prevents either loop from folding back on itself and forming a kink in the loop or the nylon. Kinks in any line are weak spots.

If your tapered leader doesn't have a pretied loop, you can tie a simple overhand loop into the thick end of the leader or, better yet, tie the leader to the fly line loop with a clinch knot (see below). With loop-to-loop connections so easy to make, though, there's a lot to be said for just buying a leader with a loop in the first place.

At some point, and probably on your first day, you'll need to add tippet material to the end of your tapered monofilament leader, so practicing the surgeon's knot before you're on the water makes sense. The surgeon's knot is ideal for tying together two lines of different diameters—in this case the end of the tapered monofilament leader, which has gotten short, and a new piece of tippet material.

Clip off about 4 feet of material from your tippet spool. Lay about 6 inches of one end of this tippet material along the end of the leader and pinch the two pieces of line together. Form a loop with the two pieces of line and pass the tippet material and the tag end of the leader through this loop twice. Tighten the knot (see illustration). Wetting the loop in your mouth will help it slip snugly together. Snip off the short ends close to the knot with your nippers and you've got your new tippet tightly tied to your tapered leader.

If you're having any difficulty learning this knot, try tying it with larger lines, say a piece of clothesline and a piece of twine. With five minutes of practice, you'll be able to tie this knot in the fading light of dusk when you'll inevitably need it most.

Note: Tapered braided leaders have a loop on both ends, and you can use a clinch knot to add tippet material. It's the same knot used to tie the fly onto the leader, described below.

Now we're out at the far end of the tippet where all the action occurs, and we need to tie the fly onto the tippet after threading the tippet, leader, and fly line through all the eyelets on the rod. It's out here that most of the knot debates focus. While there are dozens of knots with which to tie a fly to a tippet, the easiest is the clinch knot, and it works very well.

To tie a clinch knot, pass the end of the tippet through the eye of the hook, pull about 6 inches through, and then double it back on itself on the other side of the eye. Rotate the fly about five to eight times so that the loop you've formed in the tippet turns

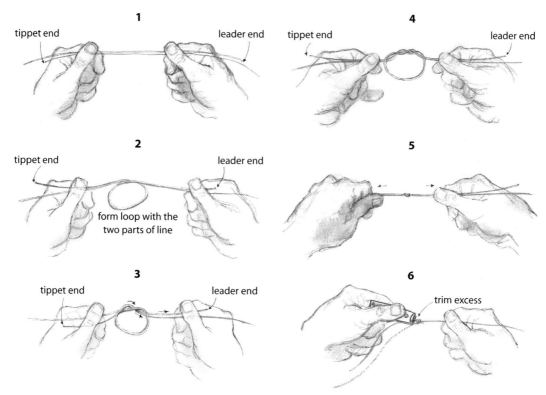

Use the *surgeon's knot* to connect lines of two different diameters, particularly when attaching new tippet material to your leader. **(1)** Overlap about 6 inches of each line and hold the two pieces parallel to one another, the end of the leader to the right and the end of the tippet to the left. **(2)** Form a loop with the two pieces. **(3)** Bring the long end of the tippet and the short end of the leader through the loop. **(4)** Do it a second time. **(5)** Wet the knot with water or saliva, and grasping both ends tightly, pull the ends outward to tighten the knot. **(6)** Clip excess from tag ends.

The *clinch knot* attaches your fly to the end of the tippet. **(1)** Pass the tag end of your tippet through the eye of the hook and form a loop by holding the tag end and the feed line with one hand. **(2)** Rotate the fly or pass the tag end over the feed line five to eight times. **(3)** Pass the tag end of the tippet back through the loop adjacent to the eye of the hook. **(4)** Holding the fly and the tag end of the tippet in one hand, wet the loop and pull on the tippet. The knot will slide down tight to the eye of the hook. Clip the tag end close to the knot. *(Elayne Sears)*

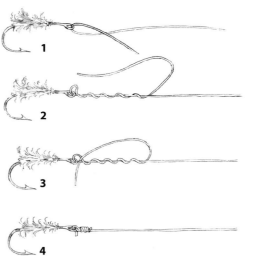

on itself. The resultant twists in the tippet will diminish the loop to a small opening near the eye of the fly hook. Holding the fly so that it doesn't untwist, pass the end of the tippet through this dwindled opening. Pull the knot tight. The twists you've made will slip down tightly against each other as in the accompanying illustration.

Clip off the end of the tippet close to the knot. Because you must turn the fly to create the twists in the loop and then pull on the fly to tighten the loop, clamping the fly into your hemostats at the bend of the hook before you begin will help, especially with smaller flies.

Now that you're fully assembled—leader to fly line, tippet to leader, and fly to tippet—let's get on with putting the fly in front of the fish.

CASTING THE LINE

If you've ever fished with a push-button, spinning, or bait-casting reel and outfit, casting a fly line will look and feel unusual. In the former you literally throw the lure, and it pulls the line off the reel; in fly casting you manipulate the line, not the lure. The two methods are completely different.

Casting a fly line isn't difficult, but it does require that you learn four distinct stages: the pickup of the line, the backcast, the forecast, and the presentation. We'll look at the backcast and forecast first.

Start out on the back lawn (or any open space) by threading the rod and pulling the entire leader and some fly line, say 20 feet, out of the top line guide. Tie a piece of yarn or scrap of cloth onto the end of the leader so you can see what the line is doing. Straighten the 20 feet of line on the lawn by walking away from it while carrying the rod. Facing the straightened line, hold the rod with the reel down, your thumb on top, and the tip of the rod pointing at the line. The rod and the line should form a straight line, and the rod should be parallel to the ground.

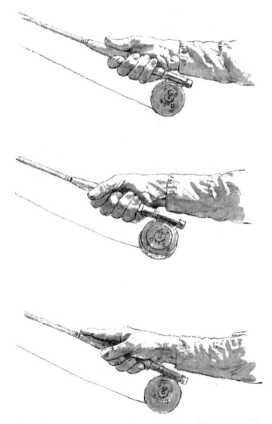

Grip is a matter of preference, though the thumb-on-top grip is most popular. *(Tom Beecham)*

Right from the start, you need to know it's the tip of the rod you'll be manipulating, and that wherever the rod tip goes, so too will the line. And it's the speed of the tip, and the way you start and stop it, that is at the core of a good cast.

Slowly begin to raise the tip of the rod, so that the line starts moving toward you. (This is the pickup of the line, which we'll discuss in detail below.) When you have the tip at about 45 degrees from the ground—or if the rod were an hour hand on a clock, at about ten o'clock—accelerate the rod tip to straight over your head. Accelerate the rod tip only quickly enough to flick the line out behind you. Abruptly stop the rod tip directly over your head, and the line will stretch out behind and above you (see top illustration next page). This is the *backcast*.

Just as the line stretches to its full length behind you, accelerate the rod tip back to the 45-degree point in front of you and abruptly stop the rod tip there (see bottom illustration next page). Again, use just enough speed on the rod tip to get the line to flick out in front of you. As the line stretches out in front of you, let the rod tip drift down to the horizontal position. This is the *forecast*. Simple enough.

Practice with this length of line for a few minutes until the line is stretching out nicely both on the backcast and the forecast. If you're stopping the rod tip on the backcast directly above your head, the line will stay high, up at the tip of the rod, and will form a nice, flat backcast that won't droop down toward the ground and won't come zooming back by your ear.

If you're not getting this nice, flat, high backcast, then you almost certainly aren't stopping the rod tip over your head. Although I'm not an advocate of telling you *exactly* how to manipulate the rod, too often what I see new casters do is to stop their arms at the vertical while

Learning to cast a fly line on a lawn allows you to concentrate on the mechanics of the cast without being distracted by flowing water. Here you can emphasize accelerating and stopping both the backcast and the forecast. You can also begin to feel the flex of the rod—the load—as the line straightens out behind and in front of you.

The proper position of the backcast, achieved by accelerating the rod tip and abruptly stopping it directly above your head. The rod then bends as the line straightens behind you, an action known as *loading the rod*.

The forecast. If you've stopped the rod tip above your head on the backcast and your timing is correct, the line and the fly will stay high over you as you accelerate and stop the rod tip on the forecast. Remember, the line will always go where the rod tip points.

their wrists cock backward as you would with a spinning rod. This puts the rod tip somewhere behind your head, nearly parallel to the ground behind you. Combat this by keeping your wrist stiff, making a single unit of your forearm, wrist, and hand. This should help you stop the rod tip straight over your head.

When you're comfortable casting this length of line, let the line settle on the ground in front of you. To make a longer cast, pull some more line from the reel with your non-casting hand—say about the length of the rod—and let it hang loosely between the reel and the first eyelet of the rod. Your noncasting hand—your line hand—should loosely grip the extra line near the eyelet, not near the reel. Start your backcast, but don't let the extra line slip out of your line hand. Stop the rod tip above your head as you've been doing, but as the line on the backcast is straightening out, let some of the extra line be pulled through your line hand. After about half the line is pulled out, hold the line tightly again for the forecast. Accelerate the tip forward, and as the line stretches out in front of you, let the rest of the line slip out. You've now extended your cast by 8 or 9 feet.

When you're fishing, this coordination of your casting motion with your line hand will help you put out exactly the right length of line and will place your fly in exactly the right spot. Lengthen the line, let a little slip out through your line hand, and make your forecast. If you haven't got enough length, start another backcast before the line hits the water and let a little more line out. This activity, making forecasts and backcasts without letting the line settle onto the water, is called *false casting* and is really an angler's way of measuring the distance to his or her target (he might also be drying his fly).

It may seem at this point that we've only worked on two steps of the cast, the backcast and the forecast. But we've actually worked on three. Back at your practice area, when you begin to raise the rod tip, the fly line easily slips toward

The line hand controls the amount of line as you false cast over water. By releasing some line on the forecast, you can lengthen your cast to exact distances. By stripping in some line with the line hand you can shorten the distance of the cast.

you, because there is little friction between the grass and the fly line. On the water, however, there is considerable friction between the water surface and the fly line. As you slowly raise the rod tip, you'll need not only to start the fly line moving toward you but also to lift it off the water. The slow speed with which you initially raise the rod tip (up to 45 degrees) will accomplish both these ends. If this sounds like one more complication, it really isn't. A few minutes on the stream makes this obvious and easy. But the action is important and is known as the *pickup of the line*.

We've actually practiced the last step of the fly cast, too. As you let the fly line extend ahead of you on the forecast, you also let the rod drift down to the horizontal position. When the forecast is finished, your rod is again parallel to the ground—or when you're fishing, parallel to the water surface. The fly is out where you want it, the line is on the water, and you're fishing. This is step 4. The whole idea of putting the right length of line out, manipulating that length, and making a good, efficient cast is to put the fly in front of the fish. Getting the fly into the fish's strike zone and getting it to look like something good to eat is known as *presentation*. And you'll find that as you become more and more comfortable handling your fly rod and casting with it, the first three steps of casting become automatic and the fourth, presentation, becomes all-consuming.

As the mechanics of casting become second nature, stalking trout and then presenting your fly effectively will take on primary importance. Remember that you're a predator on a stream and should act like one.

WADING IN

No one should step into moving water, or even still water, without a healthy respect for its power and its potential danger. Like fire, however, water when respected can become a source of companionship and joy. This short section is designed to help you develop wading skills that will keep you safe and that won't scare away the fish.

Trout streambeds vary widely, from sandy, solid bottom to muddy "grab and hold your feet" bottom to rock-strewn and slippery bottom. The velocity of the water also varies widely, as does its depth. Your first care when approaching a stream is to determine where it's safe to wade. There are no rules of thumb here, except always to use common sense and avoid unnecessary risks.

Your waders should have come with a belt or built-in drawcord to cinch tightly around your waist. (If not, get one.) This will keep water from flowing into them should you get too deep or fall in. Waders full of water will sink you. Many anglers also carry a wading staff, a long cane or pole used for stability when walking in moving water.

It bears repeating: The first time you step into the water with your hip boots or waders on, the heft of the water closing around your legs will feel as if something alive has grabbed you, the more so because your legs stay dry. The water is denser than you, and you're lighter than the water. As simple as it sounds, you need to maintain contact with the streambed and keep yourself on solid footing. The deeper you wade, the lighter you become and the more vulnerable to the stream current, even to the point where your feet may float or be washed right out from under you. Not good, because then you're at the mercy of the flowing water.

If you're swept downstream, you can avoid injury by following some common-sense advice. Because you're lighter than water, assuming your waders do not fill up, you'll float along with the current. Turn your face up and point your feet downstream so that you can breathe and see what's coming. Remember that you're floating along with the current, but the boulders in the stream are not. Your object now is to see these boulders in advance and bump them with your feet, not your head. Stay calm and drift along until the water gets shallow enough for you to put your feet down safely. Having taken a few unintended river baths myself, I can assure you that eventually the water *will* get shallow enough.

Remember when you're wading with fly rod in hand that you're a predator. The fish know this even if it's only a vague idea to you. If they detect you they'll flee or hide, and they certainly won't be

If you fall while wading in moving water, your most important precaution is to have cinched up your wading belt to prevent water from filling your waders. If you can't immediately regain your footing, turn faceup and keep your feet pointed downstream. In this position, you'll be able to breathe and to see downstream obstacles, which you can deflect with your feet.

hungry when they think their lives are in danger. Once spooked, a fish waits a long, long time before resuming normal feeding behavior—longer than you're going to want to stand motionless in your waders.

In flowing water, fish face upstream into the current. They can't see what's behind them, so that's the direction from which you should approach. But fish have other senses, especially along their lateral lines, so they can feel and hear danger. Walk lightly; don't just slog along near good holding water. When you approach a pool with a relatively calm surface, an especially attractive spot for fish, bear in mind that fish can detect you from the ripples you cause, from the grind of your feet on rocks or gravel, and by seeing

Your first encounter with the hydraulics of water will be when you step into it. Because your legs will stay dry, you'll feel the pressure of the water around them but not its wetness. When water is moving, the heft of the water makes it a force to be reckoned with. Wade carefully and stay safe.

your shadow or profile. Move slowly and carefully in the water or even along the bank; stealth just makes good sense, doubly so in still water. Act like a predator and, like a predator, move on if you've scared the fish. Once disturbed, a piece of water must be "rested" before it can again be fished successfully.

DECIDING WHERE TO FISH

Once you have some experience under your belt, deciding where to fish will be a simple matter of going where the fish are. But on your first foray with a fly rod, you want fish *and* some open backcasting space. A farm pond is nice, and many state and federal fish and wildlife agencies administer man-made or natural ponds that have backcasting space and fish, usually trout. A small lake is OK, too.

The ideal, however, is a nearby midsized trout stream, say one that averages 25 to 35 feet across. You can wade into the water to give yourself backcasting room, at the same time getting the feel of water around your legs and some experience wading in moving water. When you lay your line on the water you'll see how the current affects the drift of the fly, and you'll begin to observe what's happening in and on the water.

If you don't know where to find such a nice trout stream, look on a detailed map, ask a friend or the person who sold you your fishing gear, or call the local office of your state's fish and game department. Get on the Internet, especially the websites of the fish and game departments, where you'll often find a fishing report or a list of stocked trout waters near your home. You may be surprised how many good waters exist nearby.

KNOWING HOW FLIES SHOULD LOOK TO FISH

Trout flies! To the confirmed fly fisher, few topics resonate more richly with lore and fascination. It's a subject that can never be exhausted. We'll return to it several times in this book, and most especially in chapter 12. For our first day fishing, however, we just want to know the four basic types—dry flies, nymphs, wet flies, and streamers—and how to present them.

DRY FLIES

If you've ever noticed a bit of milkweed fluff, a leaf fragment, or even a twig floating along on a stream, you'll see that it doesn't move at all relative to the surface of the water; it's entirely at the whim of the current. Most adult aquatic insects that drift along on the surface of the stream, and that interest fish, float along this way also. Almost all the time, this is how you want a dry fly to float, too—with nothing affecting it but the current. Because your dry fly is imitating that adult aquatic insect or something like it, it needs to act like that insect, floating along unaffected and free.

The major difference for us fly fishers is that the bit of fluff or the insect isn't tied to a line, but our dry fly is. Because of this, and because the current of the stream varies, your fly line can pull on your fly, making it look unnatural. This is called *drag*.

What we're trying to accomplish when we fish a dry fly is a drag-free drift, one in which the line does not pull on the fly but instead lets it drift along naturally. The best way to accomplish this is to cast the fly upstream so that the current carries it back toward you. Your fly line will drift back at the same time and thus won't tug on the fly.

But this tactic conjures another problem, for the thick fly line floating over the fish may scare the fish. For this reason, the ideal direction to cast a dry fly is up and across the stream; that is, not directly upstream but angled somewhat across the water so that the fly floats by the fish, but the fly line does not. The invisible leader will be the only part of the line near the fish. So angle your casts. And when your fly floats past you and does begin to drag, pick it up and make another cast up and across the current.

As you fish more and more, you'll encounter many variations in how a stream's current affects the drift of a dry fly, and there are almost as many responses to combat fly line drag. We address a few of them in chapter 8. For now, however, try to get that drag-free drift.

Dry flies are intended to float on the surface of the water. The hooks are made of light wire, and the materials are attached to promote buoyancy. Nymphs are tied on heavier hooks, often with the added weight of wire wound around the hook under the materials or with beads at the head, and they are intended to sink to the bottom. Wet flies also use heavier hooks, often with wings on them to attract attention from fish. The wings also help keep the flies upright when they are manipulated through the water. Streamers are longer than wet flies and imitate feed fish. Their wings give the illusion of depth of body but also help them maintain the correct upright position when they are manipulated through the water. *(Orvis, Jim Dugan)*

NYMPHS

Nymphs are buggy-looking artificial flies that imitate an aquatic insect before it hatches onto the surface of the stream and becomes an adult. (We'll talk about hatches and emergers in chapter 4.) The natural insect itself is called a nymph, too. Usually these nymphs live on the stream bottom in and among pebbles and rocks, and you should know that the insects that are important to fish as food live underwater as nymphs for 99 percent of their entire lifetimes before they emerge, take wing, mate, and die. Using artificial flies that imitate nymphs and presenting such a fly in a lifelike manner greatly expands the time during which we can effectively catch fish.

Nymphs are vulnerable to trout as they scramble or swim along the streambed, and most of the time that's where we want to fish our artificials—down on the bottom. The natural nymphs are also much at the mercy of the current and often just drift along until they can grab hold of a rock or swim to the surface. Because of this, our best tactic for fishing a nymph is, again, with a drag-free drift and again to fish it up and across the stream, just as we did a dry fly. This time, however, the heavier hook of the artifi-

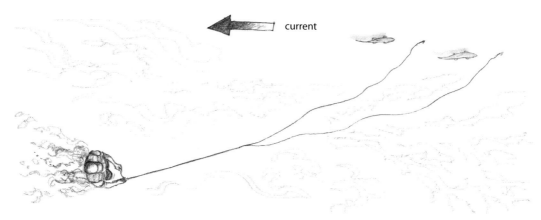

current

Casting both across the current and upstream keeps you behind the fish (which always faces into the current) yet prevents you from putting your fly line over the fish and scaring him. Instead, all the fish will see is your fly, because your leader and tippet are nearly invisible on the water.

cial and the weight that was added to the artificial when it was constructed will keep the fly on or near the bottom. At the end of its drift, as your line straightens and tightens, pause before you pick it up to recast and let the nymph swim to the surface as a natural might. Often this action triggers a strike.

WET FLIES

Artificial wet flies are designed to move and pulsate in the water. The feather wing and barbule legs on the artificial give it a lifelike attraction when it sweeps and swings in the current. Some artificial wet flies imitate actual aquatic insects, like caddisflies, while others just look alive and attract fish with their action and colors. The latter are known as *attractors*.

Because the artificial needs some action to it, the wet fly is most often fished downstream, where the current will pull on the fly line and fly and make the components of the fly come alive. As always, however, the fly line can scare a fish, so again fish it across the current, but this time across and downstream. As you'll also do with streamers, you want the fish to see as much of the wet fly as possible. You want the fly to show its full profile to the fish. Remember that fish face dead upstream, and if an attractive wet fly is swimming straight up- or downstream, a fish might not notice it.

The hydraulics of flowing water mean that most of the time the current near a streambank is slower than at midstream. When you cast your wet fly directly across the current toward the opposite bank, the faster current midstream will pull a belly into your line, and that downstream sag will pull your wet fly or streamer downstream with it, which is not what you want. By experimenting with a few casts farther and

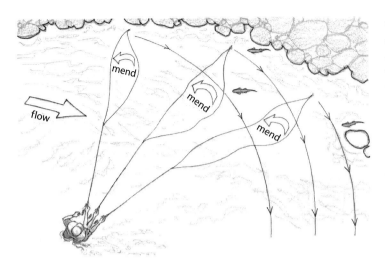

Casting a wet fly or streamer down and across the current accomplishes three important things. First, it places you on the other side of the stream and out of sight, and your fly line won't scare the fish. Second, you're showing the fish the profile of your underwater fly, giving him a good chance to take it. Third, you can adjust the speed of your fly by flipping your fly line up- or downstream (an action known as *mending* your line), thus increasing or decreasing its speed as the situation dictates.

farther downstream, you can correct this and get the wet fly or streamer to show its profile to the fish.

STREAMERS

Streamers are like overgrown wet flies except that they mostly imitate small feed fish. While the wet fly across-and-downstream presentation is also effective with streamers, small feed fish often live in quieter waters where they don't have to fight strong currents and where trout often prowl in search of them. A good presentation of streamers is to cast to the edges of these quiet waters and then give life—action—to the streamer by pulling on your fly line with your line hand. Vary speeds until you find the one that catches fish, and hold on. Often the biggest fish in the stream will be attracted to streamers.

All four of the fly varieties will catch fish in still waters, too, but in still waters fish move to find food, while in flowing waters they stay relatively stationary and wait for food to come to them. The tactics for fishing still water are not all that different. Dry flies shouldn't be dragged, and wets and streamers need to move. Nymphs are a little different, but not much. We'll discuss still waters in more detail in chapter 8.

So now you've got the equipment and fundamental skills and concepts you'll need to get on the water. You can tie knots and cast the fly line and fly. You've read some cautions about wading and have found a likely fishing spot. You've got a dry fly tied on and know how to fish it. So let's get out onto the stream.

3 | Your First Day on the Stream

"In our family, there was no clear line between religion and fly fishing."

NORMAN MACLEAN
A RIVER RUNS THROUGH IT, 1976

With your gear in the backseat of the car, it's time to go fishing. If you've had an opportunity to cast your line and perhaps catch a fish or two on a pond, all the better.

But now it's time to get onto the flowing water of a decent trout stream, where a completely new world will unfold around you. There, in moving water, the dynamics of a complex foreign environment will begin to reveal themselves. The pools, riffles, rapids, runs, pockets, boulders, eddies, and meanders of a stream or river create optimal locations for the growth of forage and optimal positions for trout to harvest this forage. Close observation will guide you to these spots. Look before you leap. As we move through this chapter, you'll begin to learn what to look for.

GEARING UP: PLANNING WHEN AND WHERE TO GO, ASSEMBLING THE FLY ROD, CHOOSING AND ATTACHING THE FLY, DONNING WADERS AND VEST

Trout exhibit peaks and valleys of activity both daily and seasonally. A trout is most active when conditions are most favorable, or more precisely when water temperatures are most comfortable. In the depths of winter or at the height of summer, water temperatures are stressful, so trout and their forage are relatively dormant. But even during the most perfect spring or autumn day, temperature variations affect trout.

Many aquatic insects that trout feed on are *photosensitive*; that is, they are affected by daylight length as well as water temperature. This photosensitivity dictates when during the year they will emerge from nymph to adult, and thankfully they adhere fairly rigidly to this annual cycle. But water temperature dictates at what time of day they will emerge.

The daily comfort zone for fish and forage changes as the season progresses. Early and late in the year, the most comfortable temperatures in the stream are at midday and early afternoon. That's when the sun has warmed the water, and before the late afternoon chill has cooled it. Conversely, as summer advances, the most comfortable times are early and late in the day, when the water is cooler.

Plan your time on the stream to coincide with these comfort zones, when both fish and their forage are most active, and you'll be fishing when opportunities are best. Fish the midday in the spring and more toward the fringes of the day as the summer progresses, then reverse that order as autumn approaches. We'll explore the effects of rainstorms, low water, high water, and other variables in chapters 4, 5, and 9.

When you park at the side of a stream, your first impulse will be to grab your gear and rush into the water. Yet a few moments preparing yourself and your gear can prevent wasted effort and headaches.

Your first task is to decide where to go—upstream or down—and how far, especially on a stream you haven't fished before. Do this by walking a couple of hundred yards or more along the bank in both directions before you gear up.

What you're looking for is the best water to fish—the best pools, runs, and holding water (as described later in this chapter), along with the best wading sections. If you're lucky, you may see some rising fish, some telltale rings on the water where a trout has taken something off the surface. Lacking that, you may spot some fish holding behind a boulder or at the head or tail of a pool—a sight guaranteed to get your blood pumping.

But keep looking. Try to see what it was that got the fish to rise. Can you see bugs on the water or flitting just above the surface? If you've spotted a trout, how will you approach it? How will you get into the water, and where can you stand to cast to that trout? Can you approach the fish at all? Developing this habit of observation will serve you well every time you approach a stream, whether it's your first time or your thousandth.

When you've got a plan, go back to the vehicle and gear up. First, assemble the fly rod. As you put the two (or three or four or more) segments of the rod together, start with their eyelets a quarter turn out of alignment. Then, just as the two pieces are snugging together, turn them into alignment. This little quarter turn locks the pieces together so that as you're casting, half the rod doesn't fly out into the stream. Look down the rod to make sure the eyes are in alignment.

Thread your line through the eyes by pulling the entire leader and a few feet of fly line off the reel. With the fly line (not the leader), form a little loop and push this loop up through the eyes. When you accidentally drop the line, probably because you're in

The ring from a rising fish tells you immediately that you have a feeding fish in front of you. While rings are easy to see when the surface is slick or smooth, on choppy surfaces these rises can be more difficult to spot. Conversely, you won't be as easy for the trout to see with choppy water, either.

Get into the habit of threading the fly rod with a loop of the fly line, instead of trying to pull the end of the leader through the eyelets. You'll ultimately save time when you're distracted—usually by the thought of nearby rising trout—and drop the line. The fly line loop will not slide back through all the eyes.

a hurry to get a fly over the fish you saw, the fly line loop will stop it from slipping all the way out of the eyes.

Check your leader to see that it's straight. A monofilament leader often gets curly from being stored on a reel, but you want it to lay out flat on the water. Just grab the leader and stretch it; the heat of stretching will take the curls out. Braided leaders don't present this problem.

Next check to see that you have enough tippet on your leader. Two to 4 feet is usually enough, but if you shortened the leader back on the lawn, just add some tippet material with a surgeon's knot.

And now tie on a fly. If you saw a fish rising and noticed what sort of bug it was rising to, pick a fly close to the size of the natural. If the fish was in relatively flat water, you should tie on one of your Adams dry flies. If the water where you'll start is faster moving with a choppy surface, pick one of your Royal Wulff flies. If you've started out with a more diverse collection of flies, try to choose a dry fly that matches the size, color, and profile of the natural you saw. (We'll talk more about fly selection in chapters 4 and 12. For now, tie on a dry fly to see how the vagaries of the current affect the drift of the fly and fly line.)

Put your waders on *after* you've rigged up your rod, slathered on some sunscreen and insect repellent, put your keys and water bottle into your vest, relieved yourself, and locked the vehicle. Parking lots can be hot, and there's no sense working up a sweat before you've even started. Cinch up your wading belt to keep water out should you fall in, then don your vest. Dab some floatant onto your fly. Some dry flies may not need floatant on the first cast or even the thirtieth. You'll figure out which ones as you go along.

YOUR FIRST CAST ONTO THE WATER

Because you've already looked at the water, you'll have an idea where to start, where the best opportunity lies, and hopefully where several good trout are holding. With a dry fly tied on you'll be approaching the fish from downstream, so either walk downstream and fish back to your vehicle or start at the vehicle and fish upstream.

Remember that you are a predator chasing after trout, and realize that most other anglers on a stream are trying to act like predators, too. They may be carefully approaching a pool, or closely watching trout before they cast, or studying insects or forage. Like predators, they may not appreciate your close approach, just as you wouldn't appreciate them interrupting you. Respect their efforts by giving them a wide berth. Don't slog upstream to them, or decide to fish close to them, or wade into the pool they are studying or working. They might react like a startled sow bear and snarl at you, or worse. (For more on stream etiquette, see chapter 10.)

When you wade into the stream, do so carefully and slowly. Reidentify where the fish was holding or at least the section of water where you think a good fish *should* be holding. Bear in mind that fish are mobile and that they can and do move as instinct directs them or as the food they're eating shifts its concentration upstream or down.

Because you'll be casting up and across the stream, work any likely-looking water near you first. If your first cast is your longest, you may well scare any fish nearer to you with your thick fly line. *Lining the fish* it's called, and it should be avoided; be sure the nearest holding water receives your first casts.

In other words, your first casts should be short casts, and these short casts give you an opportunity to see what the current will do to your fly and fly line. Because you're near the streambank, and that first cast is out into faster water, the fly will probably float downstream a bit faster than your line, meaning that it will float over any fish before your leader and fly line do. This is exactly what you want, especially when you're targeting a specific fish. Watch the fly to see how the current affects it, and once the fly begins to drag across the current, pick it up and recast.

I could caution you to be sure you have adequate room behind you for your backcast, but the first time you cast to a rising trout you'll be too excited to care. So you'll just have to learn this by hooking the bushes a few times, as did I and every other fly fisher.

YOUR FIRST CAST TO A RISING TROUT

When you're ready to tempt a particular fish in a particular spot, probably a trout that's rising to some sort of mature aquatic insect, cast your fly to the near side of where he's holding, even a few feet short of him, but upstream of his position. This is important because of the way light is bent by water. The fish can see much more of what's happening above the surface than you'll suspect, and you can scare him if you cast too close to him.

Measure the length of your cast with a couple of false casts (this will also help you keep your cast above the water, which is a good thing), then let your cast unroll above the water and gently settle down. Watch your fly and the water immediately around it. Your fish might drift up just to look at the fly or might almost take it and decide not to at the last instant. If this happens, don't just pull the fly off the surface and try another cast. Instead, let the fly drift a few feet past where the fish showed itself, then pick it up and duplicate your first cast.

If the fish doesn't show itself on that first short cast, lengthen your line a little, say a foot or so, and let your next cast drift a bit closer to him. Continue this lengthening process until the fly drifts just over his head, but not beyond him. If he shows no interest or has risen once or twice to inspect your fly and not taken it, you may need to change your fly. In this case, assuming you have an Adams dry fly tied on, you might

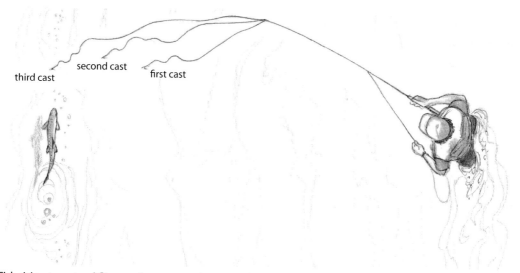

third cast   second cast   first cast

Fish rising to natural flies rarely return to the streambed after each mouthful. Rather they stay near the surface, and from this location, due to the optics of water, they can see much more than you might suspect on and above the surface. For this reason, always make your first cast to a rising fish a short one, then make successive casts closer and closer to the fish. You won't scare the fish by getting your fly line or the thick part of your leader too close to him, an undesirable outcome known as *lining the fish*.

try a different, smaller Adams. Something about your first fly isn't just right, and the problem is often solved by using the same pattern but a size or two smaller. Use the same procedure with your new fly, casting short of the fish, then lengthening out.

HOOKING, PLAYING, AND LANDING YOUR FIRST FISH

When that first good trout does rise up to take your fly, you probably won't hook him. You'll probably pull the fly right away from him, the product of trying to set the hook an instant too soon. I still do it sometimes. And then you'll say some bad words, know almost instantly what you've done, say some more bad words, then settle down and try for him again.

If you haven't nicked the fish with your fly hook, haven't had the fish feel something dangerous in the piece of food he just missed, he may well rise to the fly again. If you nicked him, he'll be wary, but at least you know you've got the right fly tied on, and chances are good that another, different fish will come to the fly.

The lesson to learn is that you need to let the fish *take* the fly—actually close his mouth around it. At the same time, however, you do need to set the hook quickly. When a fish closes his mouth around a food item, he expects a certain consistency to the morsel. If he fails to find it, the fish can expel the fly quickly. (Think of your reaction when you crunch down on a piece of shell in your scrambled eggs.)

Because this is a fly rod and not a spinning rod, setting the hook needs a brief explanation. With a spinning rod there is never any slack line between the lure and the reel. To set the hook you simply jerk the tip of the rod. But while fly fishing there will often be some slack line between the fly and the reel, the product of measuring the cast—that is, of lengthening and shortening your casting distance. There will often be a long loop or puddle of fly line on the water between your line hand and the reel. When you set the hook on a fish with a fly rod, then, you need to hold the line tightly with your line hand or press the line against the grip of the rod with your casting hand before you raise the rod tip. If you don't, the extra line will just slip out of the rod and you'll put no added tension on the hook in the trout's mouth.

Setting the hook, then, is a dicey thing. A bit too early, and you pull the artificial away from the fish. A bit too late, and the fish spits it out. But I would certainly opt for a bit later than a bit sooner, especially when your fish has moved to the surface of the stream to take a dry fly. He wants to return to deeper water quickly, and this action itself often sets the hook. But don't worry, this process of setting the hook starts to become instinctive after you've missed your first fish. Pretty soon you'll be reacting as instinctively as your quarry.

When you *do* hook a good fish—and all fish are good—the game is on. If it's a small or average-sized fish that can't hope to break your tippet, just retrieve the line by pulling an arm's length in with your line hand, holding what you've recovered against the grip with a finger on your casting hand, then pulling in some more. When the fish is at your feet, just slip your hand down the leader to the fly, unhook the fish, and watch it scoot away.

One of the advantages of fly fishing is that the fish *will* live to fight another day, because it will almost always be hooked in the lip or corner of the mouth. It will not swallow the fly (as it often does with baited hooks), thus inflicting often fatal damage. Usually, you'll be able to just slip the fly out of the fish's mouth with your fingers. If you can't—perhaps because the fly is too small or is a bit deeper in his mouth—use your hemostats. Always try not to handle the fish because you might damage his internal organs by squeezing too hard, and because handling might damage his protective coating of slime. If you must handle a fish, for a picture or to show a companion, wet your hands first to minimize damage.

When you hook a fish that may strain your tippet material to its breaking point, you need to let the preset drag on your reel do the work. Yet here again you may hook that fish when you have some slack line lying on the water.

Now you need new skills. You need to establish a direct, slack-free connection between fish and reel, either by letting the fish pull out the slack or by reeling in the slack yourself. While this is happening you can't, even for a moment, let the line go limp between you and the fish, since that would almost surely allow the fish to spit out the hook. What you have to do now is called *getting the fish on the reel*.

Releasing a fish quickly will help assure his survival. If a fish won't threaten to break the tippet of your leader, you can retrieve him more quickly by pulling in long lengths of line with your line hand.

When your fish is pulling out the slack line, you need to carefully let him take the line while still maintaining some tension on it with the fingers of your line hand. In the other case, when the fish is either not moving or is swimming toward you, you'll have to maintain tension with your casting hand—most efficiently with your forefinger pressing the line against the grip—while reeling in the excess line with your line hand. If the fish moves toward you, you can pull in slack quickly with your line hand, hold the line against the grip with your casting hand, and then pull in more line with your line hand.

When you hook a larger fish that might test the strength of your tippet, you'll want to rely on the drag system of your reel. Do this by keeping light tension on the fish with your line hand as you reel in slack line. This is called *getting the fish on the reel*. Then play the fish by relying on your drag when the fish makes hard runs. Retrieve line as the fish tires or swims toward you, but be quick to get your hand off the crank if the fish makes another run.

Most often, getting the slack line spooled back onto the reel involves some combination of all these tactics. But always keep some tension—a tight line—between you and the fish.

With the fish on the reel, the fun really starts. When the fish runs—that is, when he tries to escape by swimming upstream or down—let the reel drag keep tension on the line and fish. If it's a really big fish, keep your hand away from the handle of the reel as it spins the line out. Just touching it can break the tippet. And don't touch the line with either hand for the same reason. When the fish stops running, you start retrieving line. Sometimes this is slow and tedious—your strength against the fish's. And sometimes it's fast and furious as the fish heads back toward you.

As the fish tires he may try to get into cover, heading for undercut banks or behind snags, or he may try to wrap that darned line around something. As your experience with playing fish grows, you'll find that you can manipulate a big fish with your rod, employing its flexibility to steer the fish away from entanglements and toward you. Experience is almost certainly the best teacher here. Fish as much as you can.

If you're going to keep the fish or, more likely, want a photograph of this fine trophy, you need to land it. As I've said in chapter 1, you can use a landing net with a soft mesh, but you need to manipulate the fish and the net so that you're netting the fish either from its tail end or its side. Trying to run a good fish into a net headfirst will panic

The combination of rod flex and reel drag will give you leverage over a fish. Because the rod is limber, a fish won't break the tippet with sudden jerks or runs, and the drag will feed out line under tension. Thus, you can manipulate a fish away from snags, rocks, and strong currents as you play him.

Lead a fish toward the net and land him either from the side or the tail. While it's best for his health to keep the bag of the net in the water, it's also a thrill to show a companion your catch or to take a photo like this one. Just get the fish back into the water as soon as possible.

him into one last burst of strength, and he'll probably snap the tippet and be gone.

If you're not using a net, tire your large fish enough that you can slip your hand under him and gently lift him to the surface of the water.

With fish in net or hand, either lay the fly rod down or hold it in your armpit, and use your other hand to unhook your prize. And in all cases respect the health of the fish if you're going to release it, which I highly recommend you do. Don't yank the fish out of the water in a landing net; the weight of its own body out of the water can be damaging to an animal accustomed to weightlessness. And if you're landing the fish by hand, don't grab him and squeeze; you'll likely damage an internal organ. Instead, play him

If you decide to hand-land your fish, play him until he's tired; then just cradle him as you remove the fly and take a photo. The debate rages as to whether hand-landing a tired fish is gentler than landing him in a net that can injure his slime coating or his eyes or handle him roughly.

until he is tired enough for you to just slip your hand under him and cradle him to the surface. Don't slide or kick him up onto a gravel bar or the shore. The grit can damage his protective coating of slime. And please, no fingers in the gills or eyes.

Get your pictures as fast as you can, and then release the fish. Often he'll just swim away. Sometimes you may have to cradle him with your hands and face him into the current until he recovers enough to swim off. The successful release of a good fish is nearly as satisfying as catching him in the first place.

CHECKING YOUR LEADER, TIPPET, AND FLY BEFORE CASTING TO YOUR NEXT FISH

After you've landed and released that first fish, wade over to the shore, find a nice grassy spot or a smooth boulder, and sit down and relish the moment. After your heartbeat is back to normal and you've had a sip of water, check your leader, tippet, and fly.

First of all, carefully slip the leader and tippet through your fingers. Often in the heat of battle a fish will scrape your leader across a rock or along the bottom, creating an abraded, weakened spot. This is where it will break on your next fish. Be especially diligent on the tippet, since this is the weakest part of the leader to begin with, and any roughness or nick on it will break. If either the leader or your tippet is at all damaged, replace it.

If you find no such problems, snip off the fly and retie it to the tippet. There's no way you can discover damage to the knot with your fingers or by looking at it, so simply retie the fly, and you've got a new, fresh knot for your next fish.

Inspect your fly, too. You want to be sure that the tussle with the fish and your extraction of the hook from the fish's mouth haven't damaged or bent the point of the hook or dulled it or broken it off. If any of these things has happened, tie on another.

If your original dry fly is still functional, it probably has been slimed by the fish, which will make it sink instead of float. Wash it off in the water, dry it in your crystals, and put some new floatant on it. When it looks like new, you're ready to begin fishing again.

FISHING VARIETIES OF TROUT WATER

When you think about it, streams and rivers are just nature's way of removing excess water from the land. When rain falls or snow melts, part of the water seeps down into an aquifer, but much of it runs along the surface into rivulets, then brooks, then streams, and eventually back to the ocean, where evaporation begins the cycle anew. Water flows from higher ground to lower, of course, but it's the topography of the land and the volume of the water that together determine how fast a brook or stream flows. And these two factors can vary widely over time and from place to place.

For fly fishers, these variations translate into a wide variety of flowing water and thus of trout streams. Even a single reach of a single stream will be different each time you visit. As the volume of water increases or decreases with rainstorms, snowmelt, or drought, the places where trout will hold will change, and so must your tactics.

But changes in streambed topography produce the most dramatic variations in the flow of water. Where the grade is steep, water flows fast, forming rapids and even waterfalls. More often, however, the variations are less dramatic, the water flowing quickly here but meandering there, sometimes swirling around big boulders but at other times just gurgling over rock rubble.

Simply put, a trout stream poses an infinite variety of water types and situations, and this only adds to our fascination with putting a fly in front of a trout. Each new section of water and fishing situation forces us to stop and look and plan. But far from resenting the looking and planning, you'll find them a welcome challenge and at the same time soothing and pleasant—one more way in which fly fishing removes us from our daily cares and worries.

Stated another way, we fly fishers are looking for the locations where trout will hold, both to avoid fighting hard currents (which use up valuable energy) and to find

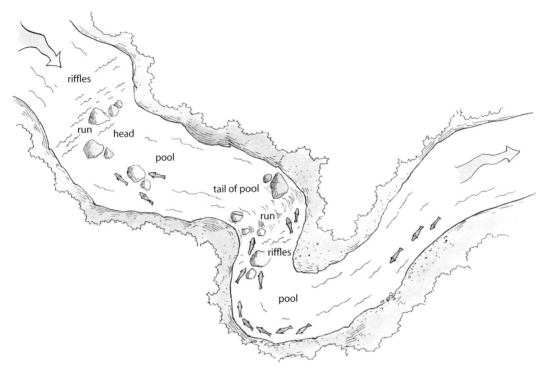

Riffles (fast, shallow sections) in a trout stream are important because they produce an abundance of forage—insects, crustaceans, and feed fish—but they offer marginal or no holding water for trout. Instead, trout wait downstream in the runs (deeper and slower than riffles) and pools (slow, deep water) below riffles where the water is safer and the current delivers the meals produced in the riffles. *(Elayne Sears)*

the food that produces that energy. This is known as the *energy equation*. A trout cannot survive if it burns more energy *acquiring* food than it derives *from* the food.

In broad terms, trout can be found in riffles and runs, in pools, and in pocket water. *Riffles* are wide sections of streams with rocky bottoms where the surface of the water is choppy. *Runs* are narrower sections where the water deepens and flows faster. *Pools* are where the stream broadens and the water deepens and slows. And *pocket water* can be found in any of these sections where large boulders interrupt the flow of water.

If we apply the energy equation to each of these situations, we'll gain important knowledge about where the trout will be holding. In riffles the stream is wide, the current relatively quick, and the water not very deep. These are tough places for trout to earn a living. Their food is usually spread out over a wide section of the stream, there is little relief from the current, and it's a dangerous place because of predators. There's no place to hide.

Often, however, riffles end in runs, those places where the water is squeezed. This squeezing makes the water deeper, but it also concentrates the food. Trout will find a comfortable spot to hold, usually behind a log or rock, and will flit out into the faster current to pick off food. Find that place in a run where the current has concentrated food near a good piece of hiding or holding water, and you'll find trout.

Pools provide just what trout need. In the depths of a pool a trout can rest in relative safety in a slow current. Good runs of water usually lead into and out of the head and tail of a pool, meaning that food will be concentrated there. Trout have the advantage of the slow, deep, and protected water of the pool in these places, yet they can also take advantage of a nearby, concentrated food flow. Bear in mind, however, that resting trout in deep water probably aren't terribly interested in food, so concentrate on the heads and tails of pools.

Classic descriptions of pocket water generally refer to large boulders that stick out in riffle water. The boulders deflect the water around them and provide pockets of still water behind them. Because the riffles do produce forage, trout can take advantage

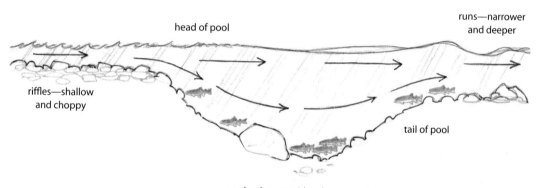

pool—deeper, wider, slower moving

A cross section of riffles, runs, and pools reveals that water depth is critical to finding trout. Riffles are rarely deep enough to provide safety from predators or strong currents, while the middle of a pool provides deep, safe resting water where trout are rarely feeding. The heads and tails of pools and the runs that feed into and out of them offer the best locations for feeding trout. The water is deep enough for safety and holding, and it's where forage concentrates from the broad riffles above a pool. The runs at the tails of pools also concentrate food, especially when the pool is either expansive, producing its own abundant forage, or small with plenty of forage drifting through it.

Pools are always alluring because we can often see trout, but they can be difficult to fish. Not all the trout in them are feeding; some may have drifted to depths because our presence has alarmed them. Also, pools are often mirror-smooth, making our presentation of a fly difficult. Better to concentrate on the heads and tails of the pools and the runs above and below them, where the fish are active and the current helps cloak our presence.

of the break in the current behind a boulder and scoot out into the current for food. You'll notice as you fish more and more waters, however, that these boulders—plus other impediments to the current such as blown-down trees, brush snags, and even bridge abutments—can be found in nearly any flowing water. They all deflect the current, and they all provide good spots for trout to hide behind and intercept food. Even where a stream takes a turn or swings around a rock outcropping or deflects off a sandbar, the redirection of the water produces a nearby piece of quieter water that is attractive to trout. Try to get a drag-free drift (also known as a *dead-drift*) of your fly along the edges of these trout havens and make it look like a natural meal.

No general description of flowing water can cover all the situations you'll encounter. Some trout streams are like long, lazy pools. The Henry's Fork of the Snake River at the Harriman Ranch in Idaho is like this. Others resemble miles-long riffles and pocket water, like Montana's Madison River below West Yellowstone. And still others come crashing out of the mountains, like East Rosebud Creek in the Beartooth Mountains of Montana, and you must search for rare spots of quiet water among the crash and froth of plunge pools. The trout are there in all these places. You just need to find them.

QUITTING TIME

Quitting time comes when your body is tired, even if your enthusiasm still runs high. No one I know can fish effectively, especially in a trout stream, for the full reach of daylight. And it's usually a tired and careless fly fisher who takes an early bath. Logic dictates that you quit before the point of exhaustion. And quit when the fish quit—in the heat of a summer midday or the chill of a late autumn afternoon.

4 | Your Second Day on the Stream

"There is no use in your walking five miles to fish when you can depend on being just as unsuccessful nearer home."

MARK TWAIN

"NIAGARA," IN SKETCHES NEW AND OLD, 1875

Soon after you start fly fishing—perhaps during your second day on the stream, as the chapter title suggests, or perhaps after you've fished as little as an hour or two or as long as a week or two—you'll begin to notice things that weren't apparent before. You'll get comfortable enough with the mechanics of your casting, your streambed footing, and the tug of the stream on your waders to expand your circle of attention, and you'll notice certain big insects that are inexplicably ignored by the trout, or rises from trout when no forage is visible, or a nearby fly fisher catching trout when you aren't. A word of warning: This curiosity and these observations signify the start of what can become a lifelong obsession with fly fishing.

WATCHING THE WATER

When fishing trout streams, you first need to find a fish. Yet your elusive quarry, obedient to ancient instinct, will do his best to stay hidden, and evolution has given him protective coloration to do just that, especially in flowing water. If there is one chink in his armor, it's his need to eat, and as I've said, the most obvious way to find a trout is to see the rings from his rises as he feeds on the surface.

Much of this surface feeding is on insects that have swum up through the water column to emerge on top of it as adults, a process known as a *hatch*. In a hatch, the underwater life stage (nymphs or pupae—see chapter 7) of an aquatic insect population swims to the surface (or sometimes walks onto dry land) to metamorphose into air-breathing, winged insects. The most critical and often the most difficult stage of this process is when the insects attempt to break through the surface tension of the water. This is known as their *emergence*, and there are specialized dry flies known as *emerger*

A rising fish like this brown trout makes obvious rings in the surface of the water, but this photo also helps illustrate protective coloration. The brown spots on the fish and his greenish-brown skin tones help disguise his presence. Note how indistinct the back half of his body becomes underwater.

patterns that imitate this phase when the insects are no longer nymphs but not quite adults.

Often aquatic insects emerge en masse to ensure that at least some of them survive the onslaught of trout from below and birds from above. A mass hatch can be a thing of wonder—nature at her most profligate—with tens of thousands of insects coming to the surface and filling the air. When these hatches occur, huge numbers of adult insects drift on and in the surface film, where they are easy, sure targets for trout.

While mass hatches are intense and short-lived, occurring for an hour or two a day and for only a few days, other hatches are more meager, with few adults on the surface at any one time. These sparse hatches, however, can last for many more hours of the day and through more days. Often these hatches are preferable, because in a mass hatch you'll have trouble getting your fly noticed, while in a sparse hatch the trout will be actively looking for emerged insects and will find your fly more easily. Always, however, you want a fly that imitates the natural's size, profile, and coloration, something we'll discuss a bit later in this chapter.

Before a hatch begins and after it ends, trout will be actively feeding on the under-

A heavy hatch is made up of hundreds, even thousands, of individual mayflies, like this one, all floating along with the current at the same time. Often, however, hatches are more meager, with only a few flies available on the surface. These meager hatches are preferable because the trout can more easily find your fly.

water life forms of their prey insects—the nymphs. The adult insect that we see during a hatch has emerged from its nymphal form in one of nature's most astounding miracles. In a brief moment, responding to a mysterious trigger, the nymph that has been living and growing for a year or more underwater swims to the surface. The middle of its back splits open, and the adult sheds the discarded exoskeleton and steps onto the surface of the water as an air-breathing organism. That's some trick.

Back underwater, there are many more similar nymphs preparing to do the same thing. As you might guess, these nymphs are as large as they're going to grow, and they're crawling out from under their rocks and moving about to find locations that favor their successful rise to the surface. Others are actually swimming to the surface. And all of them are vulnerable to trout.

By discovering which nymph is producing the hatch, you can fish the nymph's imitation productively both before and after the hatch. To make the connection between nymph and adult, you can seine the surface film with an aquarium net (another widget) and catch the nymphs just below the surface before and during the hatch, or you can simply use one of the many available streamside guidebooks to make the connection for you (see the bibliography). Regardless of how you find out which nymph imitation to use, you can be sure that trout are actively feeding on these vulnerable natural nymphs with a vengeance. Once the hatch does start, however, the trout will switch from the nymphs to the easier-to-catch adults.

In addition, trout have about a two-week memory. Even after all the mature nymphs have emerged as adults and that hatching insect is done for the year, you can use the same dry fly and nymph patterns to catch trout for another couple of weeks. Briefly put, this is because of the energy equation. Remember it? Because a single insect delivers relatively little nutrition, once a trout identifies an organism as food, he'll focus on it to exclusion and won't have to experiment with every bit of detritus that flows by. That two-week memory stays with him even after the naturals are gone,

In a mayfly hatch, the nymph completes its yearlong underwater life stage and swims to the surface film, attaches to it, splits its nymphal shuck, and emerges as an adult, the dun. The surface tension of the water is a major barrier to the insect, and many nymphs must struggle to escape their shucks and crawl up on top of the surface. These struggling nymphs, some of which never complete the process, are known as emergers. The duns then complete the cycle by breeding and dying, usually within one day. *(Tom Beecham)*

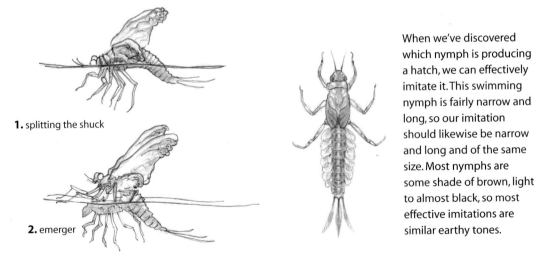

1. splitting the shuck

2. emerger

An adult mayfly hatching from a nymph.

When we've discovered which nymph is producing a hatch, we can effectively imitate it. This swimming nymph is fairly narrow and long, so our imitation should likewise be narrow and long and of the same size. Most nymphs are some shade of brown, light to almost black, so most effective imitations are similar earthy tones.

so he'll keep hitting those imitations. The trout and his fellow salmonids are ancient fish, dating back a hundred million years in the fossil record. Clearly his feeding behavior has served him well, and we've only been using it against him for the past few hundred years. It's good to remember that as you tie on your fly.

Observing and identifying which hatching insect is on and under the water, then, is a key element of trout fishing and one that will keep you interested through your entire trout fishing career. You'll hear about hatches wherever fly fishers gather, and you'll soon be offering your opinions on which hatches occur where and when based on what you've seen on the stream.

Along with your growing knowledge about hatches—and especially when the trout are not rising to some insect or other—you'll help yourself immeasurably if you develop an eye for where trout *hold*; that is, where you can find them in a stream when they aren't rising. This *stream craft*, as it's known, is the ability to assess the water and divine the most advantageous spots for trout to hide and hold.

Trout streams offer an amazing variety of structure and habitat. Knowing that fish will instinctively take advantage of their protective coloration to hide, we can begin to anticipate where to find them. Trout are dark on their backs and pale on their bellies, so you can pretty much rule out finding them on light-colored streambeds. They'd stick out there—something you and I would take advantage of, to say nothing of ospreys, eagles, mink, and otters—and trout haven't survived a hundred million years by giving their predators any unnecessary advantage. The more closely the bottom resembles the color of the trout's back, the better. In addition, trout prefer some structure—say a rock to hide behind or a log to lurk under. And finally, trout do need to eat a lot, especially if they're eating small insects.

Last chapter's discussion of riffles, runs, pools, and pocket water still holds, but to read the large variety of water you'll be seeing as a fly fisher, you need to develop an eye for the scale of these ideal situations. In small streams these hiding and feeding spots will be proportionately smaller, so don't overlook innocuous, unassuming spots. Larger waters may include pools that are too deep and runs that are too fast for our quarry, so look for smaller microcosms of ideal water—little side channels and sloughs, the back sides of islands, and small runs on the sides of bars and points. And note where you've seen rising trout for future reference. The trout won't be far away, and usually they'll be feeding subsurface.

If you take nothing else away from this discussion, remember the emphasis on *observing* what's going on around you. Actively seek out the insects that are on and in the water. Go slowly, both as a predator and as a human with superior intelligence (although there will be times when you're sure the fish are smarter than you are). Take it all in and realize that, provided you pay attention, your time on the stream will teach you more about fishing than any book—even this one.

TYING ON THE RIGHT DRY FLY

Your observations of the air-breathing insects on which trout are feeding need to be up close. It's the best way to choose an appropriate dry fly. Catch an insect if you can from the surface of the water or, failing that, look in the bushes and branches along the shore or in cobwebs. At the very least try to pick out the important details of the insect as it floats or flies by, including its profile, size, and coloration. And don't worry: mayflies and caddisflies can't bite you.

Of these details, profile is the most telling, if not the most important. Profile will tell you the general family of the insect that the trout are eating, mayfly or caddisfly. These two families constitute the majority of the surface food trout consume, and luckily they're easy to tell apart.

Newly hatched mayflies, called *duns*, hold their wings constantly upright and stand on the water on the tips of their six legs. As they drift along they look like small sailboats and are entirely at the whim of the current and breezes. They'll be inactive on the water because their wings need time to unfurl and dry. In addition, mayflies have two or three filaments or tails sticking out behind them and held somewhat erect. The artificial fly you select, then, will need upright wings, a tail, and feather barbules (called *hackle*) near its front to imitate the legs of the mayfly and to keep the artificial up off the water a bit.

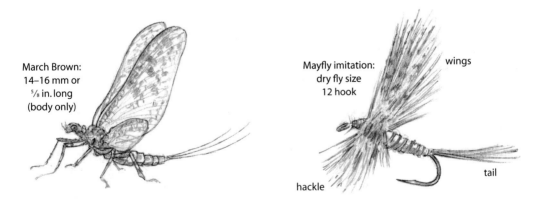

March Brown:
14–16 mm or
⅝ in. long
(body only)

Mayfly imitation:
dry fly size
12 hook

wings

hackle

tail

Mayfly duns (this is a drawing of a March Brown) are distinguished from other aquatic forage by their erect wings and long tails. Looking like tiny sailboats on the stream, they must wait for their wings to dry before lifting off the water, a cumbersome action. Their imitations, likewise, have erect wings, long tails, and hackle to imitate their legs. The structure of the artificial makes it sit upright on the water, with the hackle and tail material holding the fly in the correct orientation.

Adult caddisflies at rest fold their wings back along their bodies like little pup tents, but they're not at rest for long. They flit and jump and skate along the surface. They have two long antennae sprouting from their heads, no tails, and six legs. (*All* insects have six legs.) Easy enough. Most artificial flies that imitate caddisflies will look like this, too. They'll have feathers or deer hair swept back along their bodies to imitate the wings, will sometimes have antennae, and will sometimes have hackle to imitate the legs and help them float.

Assessing the size of mayflies or caddisflies is a bit more difficult. Logically, your artificial needs to mimic the size of the natural. On the stream you may be able just to set the artificial in your palm beside the natural and get a match, but both these families include numerous genera and species whose subtle or dramatic size variations are imitated by hook sizes from impossibly tiny 28s to lumbering size 4s. Once you've determined whether you're trying to imitate a mayfly or caddisfly, most anglers will tell you, using a dry fly of the right size is most important.

The color of the natural and its imitation may or may not be important. Remember my acquaintance who only used Adams dry flies? Adams flies are basically monochromes, comprising gray bodies and black-and-white hackle and tails mixed with a little brown, and they catch an awful lot of trout. Yet trout do see colors well, and they're sometimes very selective of the surface food they're eating, so the color of the fly *can* be important. It certainly can't hurt to match the color of the bodies of mayflies and caddisflies.

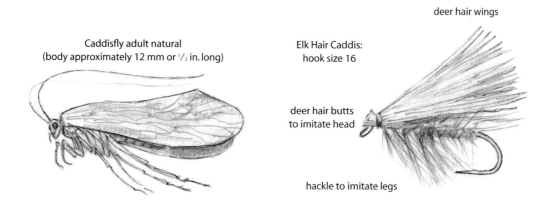

Caddisfly adult natural
(body approximately 12 mm or ¹/₂ in. long)

Elk Hair Caddis:
hook size 16

deer hair wings

deer hair butts
to imitate head

hackle to imitate legs

Caddisfly adults (here a Cinnamon Caddis) hold their wings folded along their backs, often have long antennae on pronounced heads, and have no tails. Their imitations are recognizable because of the wing imitation, which can be made of deer or elk hair, quill segments, or feathers tied back along their bodies. Hackle to imitate legs is often tied along the entire length of the body (known as *palmered*) but can be tied near the head. Some imitations lack hackle.

Are there other artificial dry flies? Yes, many—including artificials to imitate many other insects and still others that are generic, imitating nothing in particular. We'll discuss more and more of these as we progress. But mayflies and caddisflies are the meat and potatoes of trout throughout the season, and thus their imitations are the foundation of your fly box.

As mentioned, your search for the right dry fly for a specific stream at a specific time of year may lead you to enlist the expertise of a local veteran angler or fly shop owner. And there are many books that go into great detail about the insects you'll encounter on the stream: *Hatches II*, by Al Caucci and Bob Nastasi, is still the standard on mayflies, and *Caddisflies*, by Gary LaFontaine, is exhaustive. But you can catch most trout by paying attention to the details of the natural and tying on an imitation dry fly of the same profile, size, and color.

WHEN AND HOW TO FISH A NYMPH

A quick review of what we've learned about nymphs tells us that basically we should fish them up and across the current and that they're especially effective when we know what hatch to expect. A nymph that imitates the underwater natural at its maturity is always productive.

Yet we've also learned that although nymphs do take on a reckless attitude when they're preparing to make their dash to the surface, they're almost always present underwater. And trout that encounter nymphs will rarely refuse them. So the "when to fish a nymph" question can be answered by saying, "Most of the time," especially when there is no hatch to match. Even in the depths of winter or the height of summer when trout are largely inactive, a nymph drifted in front of their noses will rarely be refused.

If you're like me and find that your productive fishing time is greatly expanded by using nymphs, you'll develop a preference for a few "searching" nymph patterns to use when there isn't an imminent hatch or when you don't know what that hatch will be. My preferences are the buggy-looking Hare's Ear nymph and the delicate Pheasant Tail nymph, but you may discover others that catch your fancy.

There's a bit more to fishing nymphs than simply casting them up and across the stream. First of all, we know that nymphs need to be fished underwater, down near the streambed. In fact, many nymph imitations now incorporate small beads of brass, steel, or tungsten to help them sink more quickly. The most immediate problem is that fishing them along the bottom puts them out of sight, and unless we have lightning-fast reactions or some visual cue on the surface of the water, the fish can pick up our artificial nymph, find its texture wrong, and expel it before we know what's happening.

Searching nymph patterns are valuable especially if you're not sure which mayfly nymph is most active underwater. These flies—from left, a Hare's Ear, a Pheasant Tail, and a Prince—in a variety of sizes are productive searching nymphs. All of them can be tied with a bead head for added weight. *(Orvis)*

The most basic solution to this problem is to use a floating fly line. While sinking lines, especially sinking-tip lines, are often touted as the perfect way to get nymphs deep, they again present the problem of being underwater and out of sight. With a floating line, only the leader is underwater, and any pause or twitch in the floating fly line can indicate a strike.

Better yet, you can attach a strike indicator to the leader. Any number of widgets are offered for this purpose, including pieces of colored high-density foam or yarn or putty. You attach the strike indicator at the appropriate distance up the leader from the nymph and it drifts along like a bobber. In fact, there are even tiny bobbers now offered to do the job. When the indicator twitches, a fish may have picked up the nymph, so quickly set the hook. Many anglers swear by these strike indicators.

My own preference is to fish two flies, an indicator fly and a dropper. The indicator is a dry fly that's large enough to support the sunken weight of the nymph and is tied onto a relatively short leader. The dropper is the fly out at the end, the nymph intended to drift along the bottom. You rig it by tying a piece of tippet material with a clinch knot to the bend of the hook of the dry fly, with the nymph at the other end of the tippet. Because the leader is a bit shorter than normal, the addition of the tippet material and dropper fly affects your cast very little.

This rig accomplishes two things. First, the dry fly will twitch when a fish strikes the nymph, as any indicator should. Second, I'm offering another fly to the fish, and I'm always surprised at the number of fish that will hit the indicator fly and not the nymph. In short, I'm showing the fish two flies at the same time. I almost always catch more fish this way.

Nearly as important as seeing the strike is fishing the correct length of leader or tippet. The nymph needs to be down on the bottom. If you aren't ticking the nymph along the streambed, you probably aren't deep enough, and yes, you will lose a number of flies in logs and rocks on the bottom. But you'll catch many more trout than if you weren't deep enough. Generally, I figure two or three snags that catch the bottom for

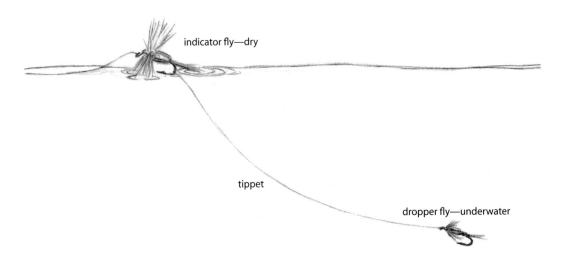

indicator fly—dry

tippet

dropper fly—underwater

To maintain contact with an underwater fly, many anglers use strike indicators, often made with yarn or putty. A better idea is to use a dry fly as an indicator, giving you a second chance at catching trout. If the indicator fly twitches, set the hook, as a fish may have taken the dropper fly. *Note:* This indicator fly and dropper setup also works well in rough water, where finding a small dry fly might be difficult. Locate the big indicator, and the tiny imitation will be close by.

every strike that catches a fish. So adjust the length of your leader often, adding or subtracting leader or tippet material.

WHEN AND HOW TO FISH A WET FLY

Wet flies started all this fuss about fly fishing. Perhaps as long as five thousand years ago they were used in Mesopotamia, at first because there weren't any hooks light enough to be floated with hackle. Yet even as recently as the early twentieth century wet flies were used almost exclusively, and they've always caught a lot of fish. Nowadays they're almost forgotten, relegated to the realm of historic curiosities, but they shouldn't be. They *still* can catch a lot of fish.

The "how" of fishing wet flies was discussed in chapter 2. You want to fish facing downstream with an across-the-stream cast, letting the current sweep the fly back across the water. If you add one more detail here, you'll learn much of the "when" to fish wet flies. And that detail is that after every cast you move a bit farther downstream.

If you do this for an hour or two, you're going to go some distance downstream. You'll be covering quite a bit of water. And this coverage is a great way to learn the details of a new stream, to discover its character and best holding water. Using the wet fly as a searching pattern, then, is an effective method.

Wet flies have a long history as productive flies. Whether they're bright attractors like the Golden Pheasant pictured here, or whether they incorporate more subdued colors to imitate specific insects like the other flies pictured here, they are moved through the water to give them action and life. *(Jim Dugan, Tom Fuller)*

Yet wet flies can also be used for specific hatches. I mentioned earlier that caddisflies flit, jump, and skate across the water. Although we'll discuss caddisflies in more detail in the next chapter, they also swim quite well under the water as mature insects, submersing themselves to lay their eggs, swimming back to the surface for air, then doing it again. Trout recognize these mature, swimming caddisflies as good food sources, and an appropriate wet fly, such as a Breadcrust, a Partridge Hackle, or a Hare's Ear Wet (see chapter 12), will imitate them effectively.

Whereas modern anglers are enamored with fishing just one fly, the old wet fly methods often involved having two, three, or more flies strung out along the leader (see illustration next page). There are other, more complicated ways to do this, but the addition of a tippet to the bend of the hook, as with the indicator and dropper setup discussed above, allows you to add as many flies as you'd like. I highly recommend starting with just two flies, however, until you get the feel of casting more of them. Three for me is about right. Just be sure to get full line extension on the backcast to avoid tangles.

WHEN AND HOW TO FISH A STREAMER

It's almost too easy to say, "Fish a streamer whenever you want to catch the biggest fish in the stream or lake," but it's true. They're the flies to use when you're targeting the biggest fish in any body of water. Yet big fish get that way by being careful, and often you need to present a streamer that closely resembles the available forage fish and behaves as if weak and vulnerable. There's that energy equation again. A big fish needs

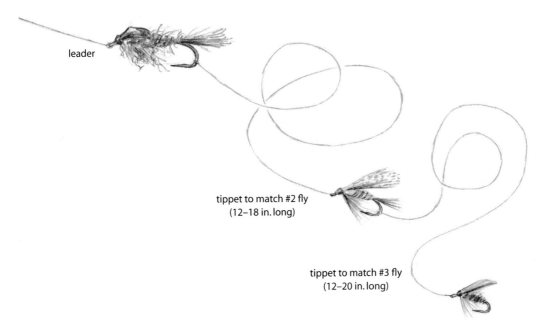

leader

tippet to match #2 fly
(12–18 in. long)

tippet to match #3 fly
(12–20 in. long)

Multiple-fly rigs are often used when working wet flies in a current. Tying successively smaller flies from the lead fly through the last dropper will ensure that the entire array casts well and fishes effectively. There are alternatives, but you can attach dropper flies by adding tippet material to the bend of the previous hook. Match the tippet material to the hook size (see table page 13) of the following artificial.

to acquire more energy from its prey than it spends catching it, and healthy forage fish in the shallows are difficult for big fish to catch.

Yet streamers do catch big fish and even little ones. Researchers have discovered that once a trout reaches 10 inches in length, it needs more calories to keep growing than it can possibly get from insects alone. It must prey upon forage fish. Thus, nearly every good-sized fish in the water has had experience with minnows, smelt, and shiners.

To repeat from chapter 2, the across-and-downstream cast is generally your best approach to fishing a streamer. With a streamer you're targeting the biggest fish, so you should be putting your fly in the most likely places for a big fish to hold. Good stream craft is invaluable. Do not waste time on spots that won't hold the best fish. Go directly to the best pools, the deepest undercut bankings, and the most fertile-looking runs.

Your time fishing a streamer, especially in flowing water, is precious because big fish are careful. They're aware of their own vulnerability in broad daylight and are most active in the low light of early morning, at dusk, and after dark. Your best chances of finding and hooking a big fish with a streamer, then, are at those times.

Streamers, like wet flies, can be bright and gaudy to attract attention like the Mickey Finn *(left)* pictured here, or they can imitate specific feed fish like the Muddler Minnow *(center)*, which looks like a fathead minnow, or the Gray Ghost *(right)*, which imitates a smelt. Again like wet flies, their construction helps them swim correctly as they are manipulated through the water. *(Orvis)*

Let's also add one or two further tactics to the down-and-across-the-stream sweep of a streamer that might better induce a strike. Healthy forage fish are difficult but not impossible for a big fish to catch. If, however, they exhibit some vulnerability, they become easy and prime targets. That vulnerability can include erratic swimming, like short bursts of speed followed by a motionless drift. Make your fly do that by pulling in some line (called *stripping in*), then letting your streamer just float in the current, and then stripping in some more line. Often, the hardest strikes will come just as you start stripping in line again.

Sometimes forage fish near death will have no idea of upstream or down. You can imitate this by casting your streamer upstream, letting it drift back toward you, and just twitching a bit of life into it. Depending on the speed of the current, this action can be easy to impart by stripping in your line just a bit faster than the current. The faster the current, however, the harder you must work.

To recap, with streamers you're after the biggest fish, so go where they're likely to hold. You're imitating feed fish, so try to use the right pattern in the right size. And try to get your streamer to look like an easy meal. Give it some erratic motion.

MENDING LINE

Mending line, as used here, is not something you use to repair torn waders. *Mending* is an action that you apply to your fly line as it drifts on the surface of the stream. You mend your fly line to make the drift of the fly more realistic for a longer length of the stream. It's a way to combat the vagaries of the current. With dry flies or nymphs, you mend line to keep the fly from being dragged unnaturally across or through the water. With wet flies and streamers you mend line to speed up or slow down the swimming action of the fly.

As discussed earlier, most casts are across the current, either up- or downstream.

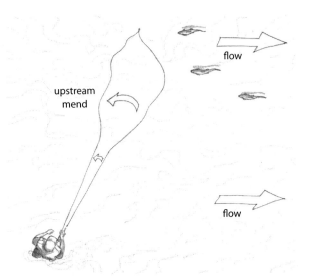

flow

upstream
mend

flow

The usual purpose of mending line is to maintain a drag-free drift for a dry fly. Mending is also important when you need to adjust the speed of a wet fly or streamer fished down and across the current. An upstream or downstream mend will decrease or increase the speed of your fly, respectively. Mend by lifting some (but not all) of the line slightly off the water and flicking it upstream or down with the rod tip.

And as you'll notice time and again, the current is not only swifter in midstream than near the banks, but it's also variable; that is, some sections of streams, such as pocket water, have several different currents across which you'll want to place your fly. If you cast straight across these currents, the swifter sections of water will quickly pull on your line. Somewhere between the tip of the fly rod and the fly, the line will travel downstream faster than your fly, and this action will quickly make your fly look unnatural. The faster currents will put a downstream bow, or *belly*, in your line.

An upstream mend of your line is the act of flipping this belly back upstream after the line has settled onto the water. It's a flick of the rod tip that picks up some but not all of the line and puts the belly of the line back upstream. By doing this you can induce your dry fly or nymph to drift more naturally for a longer time, giving it a better chance of attracting a trout.

With wet flies and streamers, you're often fishing downstream, and because you want to show the profile of the fly to the fish, you may need to alter the speed at which the fly is traveling. You can do this by mending your line upstream *or* downstream. An upstream mend will slow the speed of the fly while a downstream mend—putting a bigger belly in the line downstream—will speed it up.

When you see the need to mend line and begin to counter the effect the current has on your line and fly, you're also taking an important step toward becoming a polished fly fisher. You're progressing to the point at which your main concern is for exactly which fly you've tied on and what that fly is doing on and in the water. Your gear, your casting, your stream craft, and your approaches to sections of water will all become second nature, things you do almost without thinking. And you'll pay increasingly close attention to what the fish are feeding on, your fly selection, and how you're presenting that fly.

5 | More About Trout and How to Catch Them

> *"[The brown trout's] colour was all that can well be desired, but ill-described by any poor word-palette. Enough that he seemed to tone away from olive and umber, with carmine stars, to glowing gold and soft pure silver, mantled with a subtle flush of rose and fawn and opal."*

R. D. BLACKMORE
TALES FROM THE TELLING-HOUSE, 1896

Having progressed this far, both in the book and in your fly fishing, you're ready for the next level of understanding of trout and their environs. You'll begin to notice that brook trout not only look different from rainbow, brown, and cutthroat trout but have different preferences for habitat and forage. And you'll realize that not all streams, let alone lakes and ponds, have been created equal.

This chapter is a quick introduction to the further mysteries of the trout and his subaqueous world, a world of curiosities and complexities, of amazement and appreciation. Consider this a foundation for your further explorations. Like the rings of a trout's rise, your knowledge and wonder will keep expanding for years to come.

MORE ABOUT TROUT

In the autumn of 2002 Dr. Robert J. Behnke published *Trout and Salmon of North America*, a wonderful book by an acclaimed scientist. In it he lists sixteen species of salmonids—trout, salmon, and char—and twenty-five subspecies. I recommend the book for its thoroughness and clarity.

But for our purposes, namely trout fishing, we'll focus on the most recognizable species: brook, brown, rainbow, and cutthroat trout. All but cutthroats are found throughout the North American continent, from Canada into Mexico, wherever good trout water exists, and the cutthroats exist through much of the Rocky Mountain region and in many Pacific coastal waters. By understanding what waters are preferred by these four species, you'll know better where and how to target them.

Brook trout are actually a char, that genus of salmonids that thrives in particularly cold, even subarctic waters and includes lake trout, Arctic char, bull trout, and the Dolly Varden. Brook trout thus prefer and thrive in colder water than the other trout you're likely to encounter. In fact, they're most active when water temperatures are in the 50 to 57°F range, whereas other trout prefer a temperature range of 57 to 65°F. This will help you not only to find brookies—they'll be farther north or higher in the hills, where the smaller headwaters stay colder longer—but also to select appropriate flies. Brookies are not as selective as other trout, because the cold water they prefer doesn't support a great diversity or abundance of forage. *Finding* brook trout is your most serious problem. When you do, just put a good attractor pattern on, like your Royal Wulff. Brookies will strike because meals are meager in really cold water.

The average size for a brook trout is 8 to 12 inches, but when conditions are optimal and they have ample forage, they can grow larger. A 2-pound fish is a real trophy nowadays. In the Rangeley Lakes region of Maine, specimens weighing 8 to 10 pounds were not unusual at the beginning of the nineteenth century, but they're gone now. Brookies have white leading edges on their fins with a black stripe abutting them. Red spots on dark backgrounds pepper a brookie's sides, and their smooth skin is covered with tiny, nearly invisible scales that form wavy vermiculations on their backs and heads.

Rainbows are the most heavily stocked fish in North America because they grow faster in hatcheries than other trout and resist most diseases. They are, however, vulnerable to whirling disease, which distorts the spines of young rainbows, eventually killing them. Biologists throughout the continent are developing new whirling disease–resistant strains of rainbows and are studying methods of combating this serious threat to many fisheries. Rainbows are native only west of the Rockies but are now found throughout the continent. They are strong swimmers (indeed, migratory steelhead are anadromous, sea-run rainbows) and they prefer faster-flowing, highly oxygenated water. You can find them in and below rapids and fast runs, at the bases of waterfalls, and in fast-flowing runoff streams. Due to the large numbers produced by hatcheries they're also found in many still waters and in lesser trout streams, but the best of them require pure water, hard flows, and ideal conditions. They can be selective, but they must decide quickly whether to strike or not as a food item—or your fly—zips by. Matching the hatch helps, but they'll also readily strike attractor patterns.

Rainbows have olive- to dark-green backs and a red or pink band along each side. Black spots are prevalent on their upper halves and tails and can extend to their bellies. Their size varies depending on habitat. Rainbows living their entire lives in streams and rivers rarely exceed 2 pounds but are highly colorful. Still-water fish are

SALMONIDS

Genus *Oncorhynchus*
Pacific Salmon
    Chinook—*O. tshawytscha*
    Coho—*O. kisutch*
    Pink—*O. gorbusha*
    Chum—*O. keta*
    Sockeye—*O. nerka*
Rainbow Trout—*O. mykiss*
    Coastal Rainbow
    Redband Columbia River
    Redband Northern Great Basin
    Redband Northern Sacramento River
    Redband Sheepheaven
    Eagle Lake Rainbow
    Golden Trout, Golden Trout Creek
    Golden Trout, Little Kern River
    Rainbow Trout, Kern River
    Rainbow Trout of Mexico
Gila Trout—*O. gilae*
    Apache Trout
Mexican Golden Trout—*O. chryso-gaster*
Cutthroat Trout—*O. clarki*
    Coastal Cutthroat Trout
    Westslope Cutthroat Trout
    Yellowstone Cutthroat Trout
    Snake River Finespotted Cutthroat Trout
    Bonneville Cutthroat Trout
    Colorado River Cutthroat Trout
    Greenback Cutthroat Trout
    Yellowfin Cutthroat Trout
    Rio Grande Cutthroat Trout
    Lahontan Cutthroat Trout
    Paiute Cutthroat Trout
    Alvord Cutthroat Trout
    Whitehorse Basin Cutthroat Trout
    Humboldt Cutthroat Trout

Genus *Salmo*
Atlantic Salmon—*S. salar*
Brown Trout—*S. trutta*

Genus *Salvelinus*
Brook Trout—*S. fontinalis*
Lake Trout—*S. namaycush*
Bull Trout—*S. confluentis*
Arctic Char—*S. alpinus*
    Taranets Char
    Sunapee Trout
Dolly Varden—*S. malma*

rainbow trout

cutthroat trout

brown trout

brook trout (char)

larger and can reach double-digit weights in large lakes with abundant forage. Steelheads put on great weight and size in the ocean before returning to fresh water and can weigh 25 pounds or more.

Brown trout are imports from Europe and were first stocked in the United States in 1880. Then, as now, they filled a niche created by the widespread degradation of trout water. They do not require the absolutely pure, cold water that other trout do, though they'll thrive there. They can survive waters that are a bit warmer or a bit less pure than ideal. These survivors of Old World environmental abuses have helped restock waters impacted by New World abuses.

Perhaps because brown trout have been sought so long—they were the targets in Mesopotamia—they've also developed a reputation as the most difficult trout to entice to a fly. Indeed, they are most selective of natural forage as well as imitations. I've watched browns rise to and refuse natural insects floating down through their feeding lanes, just as I've watched them rise to my dry fly, drift along just under it until the fly started to drag, and then turn away.

Brown trout are typically brown-backed and tend to have buttery-brown sides, with dark spots on their backs and sides (and occasionally on their heads and fins) being interspersed with red spots on their sides. In moving water their average size will be 10 to 18 inches, depending on water quality and forage, but they can grow much larger.

The biggest of them are largely nocturnal, feeding actively only after dark, then skulking in deep holes or beneath undercut banks during the daylight hours. And they can grow very big. The record brown trout caught on standard tackle weighed over 40 pounds.

Cutthroat trout combine the attributes of brookies, rainbows, and browns, except that they must always have clear-flowing cold water. They can be easy to catch with attractor flies, but where they've seen a good deal of angling pressure they'll become highly selective. They'll cruise pools like browns, but they'll also relish the hard flows rainbows prefer. In fact, hybridization with rainbows is common in some watersheds, producing a fish known locally as a cutbow.

I love and appreciate cutthroat trout because many of their subspecies still have strongholds in their native ranges. There are still self-sustaining populations of Yellowstone, West Slope, and Lahontan cutthroats. They maintain a diversity that evolved over tens of thousands of years, something we anglers need to guard with rigor.

The main distinguishing feature of cutthroats is the red to pale-orange slash on the bottom of their heads, along their jaws. Their body colors vary from a light olive to a deeper green, and they may have red on the sides of their heads and the fronts of their bodies. Black spots cover their bodies sparsely or heavily and are often more numerous toward their tails. Cutthroats can grow large, especially on the West Coast, where some are anadromous, but will average between 10 and 18 inches in length.

Because of their preference for colder, almost Arctic waters, brook trout populations rarely overlap other species of trout, but often you'll find brown trout and rainbows in the same streams or still waters, although they'll separate themselves by habitat—the rainbows preferring faster, better oxygenated water in streams and deeper waters in lakes and ponds, the browns preferring the warmer, slower-moving sections of streams and the mid-depths of still water. Because of their similar habitat preferences, rainbows and cutthroats are often found in similar waters and may even hybridize. Biologists have become more cognizant of this affinity and are developing more careful stocking plans for rainbows in order to maintain distinct populations.

It's important to note that with all four of these species, the biggest specimens have come from still waters, and while still waters do pose unique problems (see below), if you're targeting trophy trout, you'll find the biggest of them in still waters and in the streams that feed into and out of them.

MORE ABOUT TROUT STREAMS

The huge variety of waters both among and within trout streams is one more facet of fly fishing's endless fascination. Identifying sections of streams that are fertile and productive is a skill that will help you every time out, and the ability to judge degrees of fertility will help you decide how to approach any stream.

A fertile trout water is one with plenty of food for trout to eat. Plenty of food means plenty of trout. Simple enough, yet this abundance must begin at the very bottom of the food chain. If there aren't any microscopic food sources for aquatic insects to eat, there won't be many aquatic insects for the trout to eat. And if there isn't an abundance of dissolved minerals in the water to support the rooted aquatic plants and algae that in turn produce the vegetation and support the microscopic plankton the insects need, then there are fewer insects, fewer feed fish, and smaller and fewer trout.

Streams flowing out of and over rocks that add helpful dissolved minerals are fertile. Dissolved minerals come from dolomite, limestone, and marble, all of which are soluble. Streams flowing over insoluble stone such as quartzite, sandstone, and granite will be less fertile.

You don't need to be a geologist to judge fertility; you just need to be observant. Streams that exhibit a well-vegetated bottom, with abundant aquatic plants and slippery rocks, are fertile. So, too, are streams with abundant hatches and numerous feed fish. Conversely, sparse vegetation or a paucity of hatches or feed fish means lower fertility and fewer fish.

On the other hand, high fertility, with plenty of forage and abundant hatches, makes for highly selective fish. You'll need very good hatch-matching skills to catch trout in fertile streams. In less fertile water the fish will be more widely spread out, but they'll strike a broader variety of flies, so basic stream-craft skills will serve you well.

In broad strokes we can also divide trout streams into freestone streams, spring creeks, and tailwaters. *Freestoners* make up a very large majority of the waters you'll fish. They're generally runoff streams whose water comes from snowmelt or rain, but they can vary from tiny upland brooks in the mountains and hills to broad flows meandering through valleys.

The smaller a freestone stream (and freestoners can range from step-across size to take-a-boat-across size), the greater the fluctuations in its flow and therefore the less fertile it will be. Lacking springs to feed it throughout the year, a small stream's water levels will rise and fall seasonally, as will its water temperatures. The fish that are present when water levels are ideal have probably migrated in and will leave again when the stream shrinks. These same water variations also affect the abundance of forage, because during low water, habitat for insects will be minimal or missing.

Larger freestoners enjoy more stable water levels, although they, too, are affected by seasonal ups and downs. But generally they have enough water year round to support both forage and trout.

Spring creeks, also known as chalk streams or limestone creeks—such as those in Pennsylvania, some in Michigan, and those in the West (as in Paradise Valley, Montana)—are miracles of fertility and production. There aren't a lot of them, but they sure are worth visiting. A

Freestone streams collect the majority of their water from rain runoff or snowmelt. They can range in size from small rills to broad flows; they can be relatively infertile mountain trickles or rivers with strong forage bases and ample, large holdover and wild trout. They can roar down the steep gradients of mountain ranges or flow leisurely through valleys. They provide a wide variety of challenges for anglers.

spring creek literally bubbles up out of the ground, usually from an underground aquifer of porous, mineral-rich limestone and marble, and some spring creeks are surprisingly full-grown and large.

Spring creeks have the huge advantages of being extremely fertile and of flowing at a constant temperature and volume year-round, so forage and trout can grow day after day and month after month. But beware: With so much forage, the fish will not only grow large quickly, they'll also be very selective. Only perfect matches of the naturals and flawless presentations will tempt these trout.

Tailwaters are something of a compromise between freestone streams and spring creeks. These are the artificial fisheries created below dams from the release of impounded water (see photo next page). They most often look just like freestoners, and you fish them as you would a freestone stream. The best of them are from water released from the depths behind the dam, not over the top. The advantage of deep-water-release tailwaters is their relatively constant temperatures—warmer than normal in winter and cooler in summer. This helps the trout stay active and growing year-round, just as in a spring creek. The disadvantage is their relative infertility, since many essential nutrients leach out behind the dam before the water is released. This often means that the forage in a tailwater fishery is minute. True, the fish will be eating year-round, and most often they will be impressive specimens, but bring a magnifying glass to tie on the flies you'll need to match the hatch.

Spring creeks emerge from underground springs born of deep limestone beds. They are rarely wider than 20 to 30 feet but are extremely fertile because of their mineral-enriched waters. In addition, because of their subterranean origins, the temperature of their water remains in the mid-50°F range year-round. These two factors make spring creeks ideal for trout growth and activity throughout the year.

Tailwater fisheries are stretches of streams that flow downstream from bottom-release dams. Because of the depth from which the water is drawn, its temperature is constant all year long. This fact alone keeps trout in tailwaters active, feeding, and growing twelve months a year.

FISHING IN LAKES AND PONDS

Fly fishing for trout—and many other species—in lakes and ponds can add variety, opportunity, and fresh challenge to your recreational angling. To target trout in still water, we can use much of what we've learned about water quality and forage from streams, including that a lake or pond needs to be both cold and fertile to support the food chains that culminate with trout.

Cold and fertile still waters harbor some of the finest trout fishing available, and for good reasons. Because we're limited to fishing from the shore or from a boat or canoe, and because the surface of a still water reveals little of where to find our quarry, it is easier for them to avoid us and grow larger. Also, the large volume of water in a pond or lake makes plentiful forage available, both insects and feed fish.

The best way to find trout in still waters, as in streams, is to see them rising to insects on the surface. Although the species of aquatic insects that use still waters are limited in number, some of them, like the famous Hexagenia mayfly, are big enough to tempt even the wariest trout to the surface. Others may be small, even tiny, but they are so overwhelmingly numerous that trout will cruise the surface siphoning in hundreds of them. Always watch the surface for feeding activity. Many of the dry flies you use in streams will be of the appropriate size, profile, and color for still waters, too.

Most of the time, however, the trout will be underwater and out of sight, making them much more difficult—but not impossible—to find. There are two critical details to remember. First, because this is still water, trout must move to find food. In streams trout pretty much stay put and let the flowing water bring food to them, but the opposite is true in still waters. Second, trout seek cold water in lakes and ponds no less than in streams. In the shoulder seasons of spring and autumn, that cold water will be near the surface. In the warmer months, however, ideal cold water will be at some level down in the water column. This level where warm and cool temperatures mix is known as the *thermocline*, and depending

Lakes and ponds hold impressive numbers of large trout but can be difficult to read because their unbroken surfaces do not reveal much in the way of structure, depth, or holding areas. In still water, trout must move to find food, unlike in streams. Yet if you learn where trout are finding their meals and their most comfortable holding areas in lakes and ponds, you'll find the biggest trout in a region.

on the size of the water body, air temperatures and turbulence above the water, and the progression of the seasons toward or away from summer, it may be at any depth, but it's usually within reach of a fly fisher with a sinking line (see illustration next page). The thermocline forms slowly as water stratifies with the approach of late summer, thickening as the depth of warm water above it increases. The ultimate thickness of a thermocline is a function of the weather and the size of the water body. Small ponds and lakes form small thermoclines or none at all if the water is constantly mixed by the wind. Medium-sized lakes will have well-defined thermoclines that rarely exceed a few feet in thickness. Large bodies of water, however, can have thick, substantial thermoclines.

So you need to find the depth of the thermocline. Within it and along its top or bottom fringes is where the trout will be making their living and where you need to put your fly. (A dark Woolly Bugger or an attractor streamer like a Mickey Finn is an excellent choice for still-water searching flies.) Use a sinking fly line and note the depth at which you begin to catch trout (see below for details); you'll have discovered the thermocline. Keep fishing at this depth for the remainder of the day, and you should keep catching fish.

In essence, you do your best to read the water in lakes and ponds just as you do in streams. Most of the time you'll need to discover what the trout are feeding on, insects

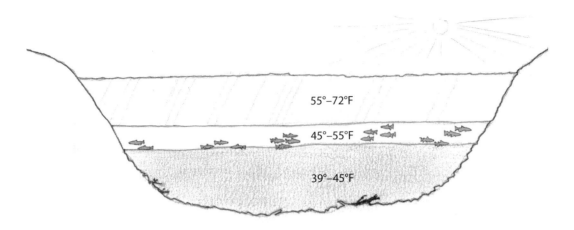

55°–72°F

45°–55°F

39°–45°F

The thermocline, where trout make their living during the dog days of summer, is formed in medium to large lakes when air temperatures and sunshine raise the temperature of the surface waters. Colder water sinks, and warmer water floats, and the area of mixing between these two is the thermocline. It attracts trout and forage because it isn't too warm, as the surface would be, nor too cold, as the deeper water would be. The thermocline is thicker and more distinct on larger waters, thinner or missing altogether as waters get smaller and shallower.

or other forage, and where they are finding that forage, often within the thermocline. But there are other areas of lakes and ponds that attract and hold trout, namely the inlets and outlets of these waters and any upwellings of groundwater, or springs, within them.

Inlets concentrate trout at certain times of year when food concentrates there. Sometimes stream-born insects will drift down into the lake, attracting trout either because the insects are forage or, often, because the insects attract smaller feed fish that in turn attract trout, and often large trout. In addition, some species of forage, such as rainbow smelt, migrate up into streams to spawn in the spring of the year. They will gather at the mouths of inlets to wait for just the right water volume and tempera-ture to proceed, and the trout will feast on them there. And in summer, inlets often sup-ply a welcome slug of colder water, again an attraction to forage and to trout.

Outlets are a bit more complex. Feed fish venture into and back out of streams in pursuit of the larger variety of insect forage there, and trout will often gather at the out-lets to intercept these smaller fish. In fact, the trout themselves often migrate from lakes down into streams for the insects. In addition, most stream-born mature aquatic insects will fly upstream to combat the effects of flowing water. If they didn't, all the adults would end up far downstream. And finally, many forage species spawn in flowing wa-ter by heading downstream instead of up, returning to their still-water homes when

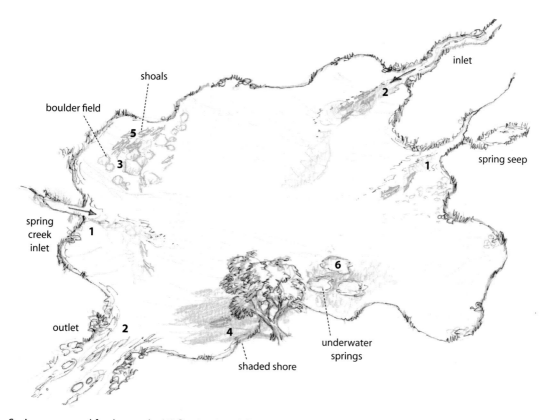

Spring seeps and feeder creeks **(1)** flowing into lakes and ponds provide ideal water temperatures regardless of the time of year, so identify these areas and concentrate on them. Inlets and outlets **(2)** concentrate forage and attract trout, too. Yet trout move in still water and can also be found foraging in other areas of a lake, such as in boulder fields **(3)**, along shaded shores **(4)**, on shoals where feed fish might concentrate **(5)**, or around underwater springs **(6)**.

they have laid and fertilized their eggs. Thus, both the returning forage and their offspring swim upstream to the lake, and trout lie in wait for them at the outlets.

Underwater springs are especially important when temperatures in the lake at large become uncomfortable to trout. The trout will home in on the cold water of the spring, as will much of the lake's forage. These springs become summertime meccas; the trick is to identify where they are and then take advantage of them.

Finding springs can be as easy as trailing your hand on the water as your canoe cruises a pond. You'll *feel* the temperature change. More effectively, you can watch for them. Just sitting still and looking will often reveal a smattering of surface activity characteristic of small feed fish, which are near the bottom of the food chain but at the top of the pond. They prefer colder, deeper water, too, but the big fish that are down deep force the feed fish to the surface. Find these small fish dimpling the surface, and you'll find larger fish below them. And you'll find the biggest fish right down near the bottom, basking in the comfort of the spring seep.

When trout are rising to hatching insects on the surface of a lake or feeding on nymphs near the surface, your standard floating line, leader, and fly rig will be ideal. Just remember that the trout are moving, not the water, so you'll need to guess in which direction your trout is swimming, then lay your fly out in front of him and let it sit there. No drag on the fly, please.

When the fish are deeper, you'll need a sinking fly line (see chapter 1) to get your fly down to them. Most sinking fly lines nowadays come *density compensated*, meaning that the entire line will sink at the same rate regardless of its taper. This wasn't always the case. Formerly, if you were fishing a weight-forward line, the thicker-sectioned line out at the end would sink faster than the rest, and you'd be fishing at the desired depth only for a short time. With a density-compensated line, your entire fly line sinks at the same rate and keeps your fly at the preferred depth while you're stripping in line and until you must pick it up and recast. Vary the speed at which you retrieve your fly until you discover the speed that attracts strikes.

A density-compensated sinking fly line also comes with a specified sink rate, usually given as so many inches per second, as in 3.5 inches per second. Try to remember this sink rate so that you know how deep you're fishing. Even if you can't remember

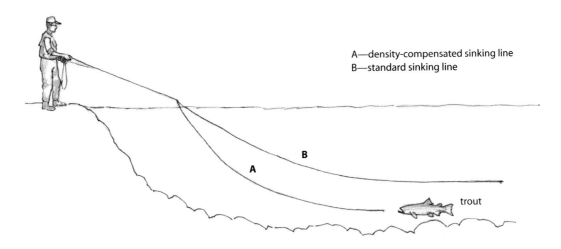

A—density-compensated sinking line
B—standard sinking line

trout

Because density-compensated line sinks at a uniform rate, all of it will be at your intended depth when you retrieve it until you get your fly close to you. Standard sinking line will sink faster at its tip and will be retrieved at an angle, meaning that it's within the effective area where trout are holding only for a short time.

the rate, count the seconds of sinking. That way, when you start catching fish—usually within the thermocline—you can get your fly line back to the same depth.

Most subsurface fishing is done with a wet fly, a swimming nymph, or a streamer. Each of these flies needs motion; that is, it needs to appear alive, as if swimming through the water. Flowing water will stir a fly to life if you just hold the fly stationary against the current, but in still water you must move the fly to give it life.

You can, of course, do this simply by trolling the fly—running your line out behind your canoe or boat and then paddling or motoring around in search of fish. Some states, such as Maine, do not permit a fly to be trolled in fly fishing–only lakes, raising a debate about whether trolling is really fly fishing. But that's a debate for another time and place.

Often, however, especially when you're targeting a specific section of a pond or lake, you'll need to give motion to a fly by casting it out, letting it sink to the desired depth, then stripping in line to make the fly look lifelike. Vary the depth to which you allow the fly to sink, the speed with which you retrieve the fly, and the places where you cast your fly until you've found fish. Where you find one, there will probably be more.

Now you've got the basics of fly fishing under control. You know something about the various rods, lines, and equipment, and you've assembled and used them. Hopefully you've caught a few fish and have begun to observe trout and the waters in which they live. You've begun to select flies and can present them so they look natural and enticing on and in the water.

Now it's time to address some of the bumps you've encountered along the way: casts that went awry, good trout water where you just couldn't cast at all, and situations on the water that cried out for more information.

Most of all, by this time you've probably had days on the stream when you should have been catching fish but weren't. Perhaps the fish ignored every fly you showed them, or perhaps they were feeding actively on the surface but on nothing you could see. Much of the frustration of fly fishing is like that. We know our timing is perfect, our presentation is good, and we've got trout in front of us, but we just can't buy a strike.

I try to minimize those times by continuing to learn about what trout eat, how best to imitate those myriad insects and forage species, and how best to present my imitations. It's what all true fly fishers do, and I hope I can help you do so, too. Much of your fly fishing from now on will aim to expand what you know about trout forage, how trout see and use forage, and how best to imitate it.

It's time for part 2.

PART TWO

THE ART
AND SCIENCE
OF FLY FISHING

6 | Casting Problems and Solutions

"Never throw with a long line when a short one will answer your purpose."

RICHARD PENN
1833

In a perfect world—say on your back lawn on a sunny day with no wind—casting problems are minimal. The four stages of the cast discussed in chapter 2 are simple and straightforward. In the real world of trout streams, however, things are different. In addition to the varieties of water types and situations already introduced, you'll encounter bankside bushes, overhanging trees, up- and downstream winds, in-stream logs and boulders, bird life to watch, insects and rising trout, and myriad other things to distract, delight, or confound you. As you become more and more observant of what's happening in, on, and around the water, the last thing you're thinking about is the details of your cast. And problems *will* crop up.

The following list of problems and their solutions is not exhaustive. These problems, however, are the most common ones faced by fly fishers, and their solutions will help you solve most other problems that might occur.

THE LINE DOESN'T STRAIGHTEN OUT ON THE BACKCAST OR THE FORECAST

When I discussed the pickup, the backcast, and the forecast in chapter 2, I emphasized accelerating the rod tip, then quickly stopping that acceleration. A closer look at what's happening during these actions will enable us to straighten out both the backcast and the forecast.

Remember that during the pickup we're slowly raising the rod tip and getting the line moving toward us and up off the water. This effectively takes all the slack out of the line, or should. We need to get the slack out so that the entire line moves at the same speed during the backcast. If it doesn't, bad things happen, like big loops and tangles. So again: Don't start accelerating the rod tip until all the slack is out of the line, the line is moving toward you, and it is beginning to break the surface tension of the water.

That's when rod tip acceleration will get the line entirely off the water and headed backward without loops and tangles.

As we accelerate the rod tip during the backcast, the rod bends. Remember that acceleration means increasing the speed. We're not trying to get the rod tip up to a certain perfect speed and then maintain it. Rather, we keep increasing the speed until we stop it abruptly at the top of the cast. This acceleration puts an increasing bend in the rod, known as *loading the rod*. When we stop the acceleration abruptly, the bend begins to straighten, or *unload*, throwing the line backward on the backcast or forward on the forecast.

If the line doesn't straighten out on the backcast or forecast, we haven't accelerated sufficiently to put enough *load*, or energy, into the bend of the rod to throw the line all the way back or forward. Our acceleration of the rod tip, and thus the line, needs to be quicker. The rod needs to bend more.

The main problem with increasing the acceleration of the rod tip is that most people then miss the stopping point at the top of the cast. In their zeal to get the rod tip going faster, they propel the rod tip farther behind or down in front of them than they should. Then, not only will the line not straighten out, but it will probably hit the ground or the water behind or in front of them, making a puddle of line. Remember, increase the speed of the rod tip, but stop it at the top of the cast.

Step 1 of casting a fly line is the pickup, as mentioned in chapter 2. In it you raise the rod tip to about 45 degrees above horizontal. This action accomplishes two things. First, it gets the slack out of the line, thus enabling you to control your backcast with a tight loop. Second, it breaks the surface tension of the water. If you don't do this before you accelerate the rod tip to the vertical, you'll overpower the backcast, and the line will snap back at you.

THE LINE CRACKS LIKE A WHIP

If you've been out fishing a few times, you've probably heard a whip crack behind you. You've probably then made a few more casts and eventually noticed that your fly was missing, caught in the bushes you guessed. Nope. You've literally cracked the whip—made a little sonic boom with your fly line that exploded your fly off into fly heaven. I still do it after forty years of fly fishing, usually because there's a good fish in front of me and I'm too impatient to let the line straighten out all the way behind me.

That's the key to the problem. If your backcast doesn't straighten out behind you before you start the forecast, then your fly is still going backward as the fly line is coming forward, effectively doubling the energy that hits the fly when its backward motion gets hit with forward energy. Kaa-snap!

The absolute truth about casting a fly line and fly is that it's all about timing. Backcast, pause, forecast. If the pause is just a wee bit too short, the whip crack occurs, and your fly is heading heavenward. If the pause is a bit too long, the line on the backcast begins to drift down and will catch the bushes.

Practice will help, but practice on the stream. Casting on the back lawn is fine when you begin to learn, but it gets boring quickly. Make yourself think about the cast on the water when you're doing it, then worry about catching fish. It's much more fun.

Eventually, you'll be able to feel when you've made a good cast: good backcast, per-

Timing on the backcast is critical. The line must straighten out before you begin the forecast, and you must begin the forecast just as it does. If you wait too long, the line will drop and come zipping back by your head; most people make this mistake only once or twice. More common is starting the forecast too soon, as here. The usual result is a whip crack and a vaporized fly.

fect pause, good forecast. This is not some mystical experience. It's just your eye-hand coordination literally feeling the rod loading and unloading. You'll feel, through the rod, when it has come back straight on the backcast and then reloaded, or arced, on the forecast. As the line straightens out beautifully in front of you, you'll know that your pause was exact and perfect. As you cast more and more, this coordination will become second nature for all the lengths of line you'll need. So to become an effective caster, you need to fish more. That's as good an excuse as I can think of to go fishing.

UNWANTED KNOTS IN THE LEADER: THE TAILING LOOP

A tailing loop is a frustrating thing. You're fishing along, you need to make a longer cast, and somehow your fly ends up tangled in either the leader or tippet, or, more often, you later discover an unwanted knot in your leader. The physical explanation of this phenomenon is that your fly crossed paths with your fly line; that is, somehow the fly got lower on the way back than the fly line and crossed it. Then, when you started your forecast, the fly created a loop in the fly line that ended in the tangle or knot. The key elements here are that the fly was lower on the backcast and that it crossed the fly line.

Theories abound on how to fix this problem. One is that you're dropping your hand a bit when you start the forecast, thus lowering the fly line (remember that the line

Tailing loops are mysterious gremlins, difficult to combat. We know they occur when the fly falls below the fly line on the backcast, often resulting in tangles of line or, at the very least, unwanted knots in the leader.

goes where the rod tip goes), and crossing the lines into the tailing loop. The cure according to this theory is not to lower your hand that tiny bit, but for me that's nearly impossible. I'm not consciously dropping my hand in the first place, so how can I consciously *not* drop it?

For me, the solution to the effect of the tailing loop is to get the fly out of the way in the first place. Because a tailing loop results when the fly is both lower than the returning fly line *and* across it, I consciously make my backcast a bit off to the side, canting my rod tip a few degrees from the vertical plane that bisects my body. Then on the forecast, I bring the rod tip back right over my head in that vertical plane. This action puts the fly off to the side a bit on the backcast and then brings the line and the fly on the forecast right over my head. The line and fly can't cross and can't form a knot or tangle. I suspect this doesn't eliminate the tailing loop, but it does eliminate the *effects* of the tailing loop.

backcast

forecast

THERE'S NO ROOM FOR A BACKCAST

In many streamside angling situations, you're going to find there's no room behind you for a backcast. Perhaps the bushes are too close or too tall, or the stream itself is too narrow. But there are good trout out there where you want your fly to be, and, happily, there are tactics to help you get your fly to them.

The most common tactic in this case is to use a *roll cast*, which takes advantage of the surface tension of the water to eliminate the need for a backcast. Here's how to do it:

First, eliminate any slack in the line by raising the rod tip. The line will start sliding along the surface toward you as in the pickup for a backcast, but don't accelerate into a backcast. Instead, keep raising the rod tip to the vertical position

One solution for tailing loops is to angle the rod tip away from your body on the backcast and then bring the forecast straight over your head. While the fly may still fall below the plane of the line, it will be out to the side and thus won't entangle the line.

The roll cast is especially useful when there's no room for backcasting. By bringing your rod tip just beyond vertical behind you and letting the line on the water stop moving, you create a roll cast merely by making a standard forecast. The magic of the line looping out over the water is provided by the surface tension of the water preventing the line from scooting back toward you.

and a little past it. When the line stops moving toward you but is still resting on the water, make a standard forecast. Accelerate the rod tip back down to the ten o'clock position, about 45 degrees above horizontal, and stop abruptly. The line will miraculously roll out above the water.

If you want to practice this cast on the back lawn, you'll need to have someone stand on the tippet end of the line to imitate the way the surface tension adheres to the line. Then make that standard forecast and watch in amazement as the line loops out. What's happening—on the lawn and on the water—is that the energy you've put into the cast translates into picking up the line and resetting it. You'll notice that the loop of line runs right out to the end, in the process moving the line just where you want it. When you're on the stream, the line does *not* slip along the water back toward you. And because the loop will travel in the direction of the rod tip, you can make the line move upstream or down. Just aim your forecast in the direction you want to go. It's a great cast when you're wading along the shore of a lake or pond, too.

There are a couple of important details. The first is that you can't let the loop catch on itself. To combat this, tip the rod *away* from the line that's lying on the water and *to-*

To practice the roll cast on grass you need an assistant to stand on the tippet of your line. This imitates the way the surface tension of water holds onto the line, something that grass and dry ground can't do.

ward your target. If the target is to the right of where your line is lying, tip your rod tip to the right and make your roll cast. If it's to the left, make your roll cast to the left. This action allows the loop to pick up the line and carry it toward your target without hitting itself and collapsing (see illustration opposite).

It's also important that the tip of the rod stop high enough on the forecast to keep your rolling loop above the water. As we've said, you should cock the rod tip back to and beyond the vertical at the start of the cast so you'll have enough room to get the rod up to speed on the forecast while still stopping it above 45 degrees. Experiment with taking the rod tip farther and farther behind you to start the cast. Just be sure that you stop it high enough on the forecast to get the loop above the water.

CASTING SINKING LINE AND HEAVIER FLIES

The biggest problem with casting the sinking lines that you'll use mainly in still water is that, well, they sink. If you try to cast them while they're still underwater, you'll need way too much force to get the line airborne on the backcast. By the time the line gets fully stretched out on the backcast, it will be moving so fast that it will recoil toward the back of your head before you can make your forecast. The resultant slack will cause your forward cast to collapse and land in a heap.

The solution involves going back to the first step of a basic cast, the pickup. With a floating line, everything is happening on top of the surface, and you can see that the pickup is designed to get the line off the water. You then accelerate the rod tip and the line into the backcast. You need to do the same thing with sinking line; that is, you need to get the line up onto the surface of the water and airborne *before* you begin your backcast.

This isn't as difficult as it sounds. With a sinking line, you're using a fly that needs motion—a streamer, wet fly, or nymph that you manipulate by stripping in line to make the fly look lifelike. As this stripping motion gets the fly close to you, the sinking line and the fly will be near the surface, the length of fly line still in the water will be quite short, and you'll be able to get it the rest of the way to the surface by raising your rod tip as you always do in the pickup to start your backcast. The line you stripped in will lie loosely at your feet, and you can then false cast this excess line out to the distance you want, just as you would a floating line. The key is to get the line up out of the water and into the air as you start your backcast.

You may also want to use sinking line, or at least a sink-tip line, in certain

On a roll cast, angle the rod tip away from the line that remains on the water, up- or downstream depending on where you want to reset your fly. If the rolling loop of line is directly over the line on the water or crosses it, the loop will collapse as it hits the line being picked up.

flowing water situations. Casting the line in these situations is a bit easier. Because the water is moving, when the line straightens out in the current it will begin to rise to the surface. You may need to strip in some line to get all of it to the surface, but once it is on top, you cast it as you would any floating line. Again, the pickup of the line is vital. You need to get the line into the air as you start your backcast, but this will be easier because of the help you're getting from the flowing water.

Heavier flies, those big streamers and swimming nymphs that catch big fish, present the same problem as sinking lines, and the solution is also the same. You need to get that big fly up onto the water surface and then off it before you begin the power stroke of the backcast, and you do it the same way whether you're using sinking or

The secret to casting sinking or sink-tip lines or heavier flies is to get the line and the fly out of the water and into the air. You do this by stripping in enough line to get it on top of the water and then making a standard cast. The cast itself will look and feel exactly the same—same backcast, same forecast.

floating line. Strip in enough line fast enough to get the fly near the surface before you start the backcast, then cast as you always do.

It's important to note here that sink-tip, sinking, and floating fly lines of the same weight designation do, in fact, weigh exactly the same. That is, within the first 30 feet, a 6-weight floating line weighs the same as a 6-weight sinking or sink-tip line. The difference is one of thickness, with a 6-weight sinking line having a smaller diameter and a higher density. Once you get any 6-weight line airborne, it will load the rod the same way, requiring the same backcast and forecast to complete the cast. You don't need to increase the power of the cast with a sinking line; you just need to get it up off the water.

CASTING IN THE WIND

When the wind comes up while you're fishing on a stream or still water, it can be a nervous time. You'll feel, at first, as if you can't control where your fly is going during the backcast and forecast. A gust at the wrong time, and you might find that Royal Wulff impaled in the back of your neck (or at least in your shirt collar if you were careful enough to turn it up).

Yet the wind doesn't have to blow you off the water. Short of a gale in which you'd have trouble staying upright yourself, you can keep fishing when the wind is blowing and can maintain control of that light line with good rod handling and casting techniques. You can manipulate your rod and line so that your fly not only is not a danger to you but also goes where you want it to.

If the wind is blowing at you, you'll need more rod tip speed and a very abrupt stop in your forecast. This will close the loop of the cast, making it very tight, and the line will travel quickly out. Conversely, when the wind is from behind, you need more acceleration and a quicker stop on your backcast. In essence, you're quickening the cast to overcome the speed of the wind.

In addition, try a high backcast with a wind in your face or a high forecast with a wind from behind. In either instance the quick cast of a tight loop into the wind will keep the line down low, where the wind doesn't have the opportunity to blow the cast apart. That is, if the wind is blowing from behind you, accelerate and quick-stop your backcast into the wind so that the line straightens out close to the ground or the water. You do this by starting the acceleration of the backcast with the tip higher up than normal, just shy of the vertical, and stopping it farther behind the vertical than normal. The arc of the cast will then make the backcast run out closer to the water or ground behind you. Then come over the top with a standard forecast, which will describe a higher angle over the water by virtue of its lower than normal start. The tight backcast will straighten out into the wind, and your forecast will go where you aim the rod tip. You must have room behind you to make this cast—that is, no bushes or banks to catch your low-arcing fly, and it will help if you shorten the line for the backcast. Strip in more line than usual for your backcast, make a tight, fast backcast, and then let the wind pull out the excess line on the forecast.

With the wind at your back, you want to get your backcast lower—"under the wind," some would say. Do this by starting the acceleration of your rod tip higher up than usual, approaching vertical. This means that you'll stop the rod tip farther behind your head, which will cause the line to stay low behind you. On the forecast, do exactly the opposite, starting the acceleration of the cast from the lower rod tip position and stopping the rod tip near the vertical. The line will roll out higher than usual; let the tip drift down to its normal position for your presentation.

CASTING PROBLEMS AND SOLUTIONS

Symptom	Problem	Solution
Line has big loop or doesn't straighten out entirely on backcast or forecast	Insufficient acceleration	Load the rod more by increasing acceleration, then stopping abruptly overhead on backcast, or at 45 degrees on forecast
Line drops to water or ground on backcast	Not starting forecast soon enough	Start the forecast just as the line straightens out on the backcast
Line cracks like a whip	Starting forecast too soon	Let the line straighten out on the backcast before you start the forecast
Tailing loop or knots in the leader	Fly is crossing the fly line	Angle the rod tip to one side on the backcast and bring the forecast straight overhead
Fly line hits rod on forecast	Forecast is neither above nor to one side of rod tip	Angle the rod tip to one side on the backcast, then bring the forecast straight overhead; be sure to bring the tip down to 45 degrees
Line has unwanted S-curves on forecast	Insufficient acceleration on backcast	Use more acceleration to get the backcast to straighten out behind you
Backcast is fast and flat enough but too low	Ending backcast with rod tip too low	Stop the rod tip sooner on backcast so it doesn't drift too far down behind you; the line will follow
Roll cast lands in a pile	Ending forecast with rod tip too low	To stop the rod tip on a roll cast at the twelve o'clock position, you must start the forecast with the rod tip farther down behind vertical
Loop on a roll cast hits the line and collapses	Errant aim	The loop must not cross the line as it rolls out, so keep the rod tip on the same side as the loop—left or right—on the forecast

Symptom	Problem	Solution
Difficulty casting sinking lines or heavy flies	Failure to overcome surface tension of water on pickup	Strip in line until it and the fly are on top of the water and free of surface tension, then cast normally
Sinking line or heavy fly doesn't roll out as it should on forecast	Starting backcast too soon	Start the backcast only when the sinking line or heavy fly is free of surface tension of water
Wind from behind messes up backcast	Failure to adapt with a tight, low backcast	Start the backcast with the rod tip higher than normal, and stop it farther behind you so the line rolls out low; it may help to shorten the line for the backcast and let the wind pull out excess line on the forecast
Wind from in front messes up forecast	Failure to adapt with a tight, low forecast	Start the backcast with the rod tip lower than normal, and stop it sooner so that the line rolls out high behind you; then make a tight, low forecast into the wind
Wind from the side ruins the cast	Keep the cast downwind of your body	Cast over your downwind shoulder or with your downwind hand

Likewise, with the wind in your face, make your backcast, which is now with the wind, at a higher angle than usual by starting it with your rod tip closer to the water than the usual 45-degree angle and ending it shy of the vertical. Then make that quick acceleration and stop of the forecast into the wind, stopping the rod tip closer to the water than 45 degrees, so that the line scoots out just over the water—"under the wind." The added acceleration makes a very tight loop, and it unrolls just above the water.

With just a little practice, these two new components of casting—the quicker, tighter loop and the new angle of the cast—will overcome any facing or tailing wind.

Side winds are a bit different, but they're easier to solve. When the wind blows from your casting-hand side, it wants to blow the line and fly into you. If you try to solve this problem by casting higher to keep the line above your head, the wind will have a field day with your line, and you'll lose control of how and where the line settles down onto the water. So your first commitment is to make the same cast you normally would—or even better, to keep the line low to the water, under the wind.

Yet the wind will still tend to blow the line into you, so the best solution is to make your standard cast, but make it from your downwind side. That is, angle the rod across your body so that the tip and line are downwind of you for both the backcast and forecast. Any wind effect on the cast will blow the line *away* from your body, not *into* it.

An even better solution is to use your other hand. Practice casting with your nondominant hand. Then, no matter which side the wind is coming from, you can keep the line blowing away from you.

OK, I know this sounds like I'm asking you to be ambidextrous after you've just gone through some pretty strenuous practice to get proficient when casting with your dominant hand. But nobody is more right-handed than I am, and the

With a crosswind blowing from your line-hand side, you merely need to add a bit more power to your cast to combat the wind. If the wind is blowing from your casting-hand side, simply angle the rod over your opposite shoulder and again add a bit of power to combat the wind. Because the rod tip is now on your line-hand side, any underpowering of the cast leaves the line drifting harmlessly away from you.

idea seemed a bit ludicrous to me, too. Yet when I was away from everybody else on a stream one windy day, I tried it, and in a half hour I could cast effectively with my left hand. No, I was not as precise, nor did I cast with as much authority as I could with my right hand, but I did cast well enough to catch fish. And as an added plus, many times when I'm fishing along a stream I find myself on the wrong side. I want to cast upstream close to shore, but my right hand is the shore hand. Now I just switch over to my left hand, have casting room out over the water, and can put a fly into a pocket of water right next to the riverbank. It's a big help.

7 | More on Understanding and Imitating What Trout Eat

"She yielded to the lunacy of angling, not by slow degrees (as first a transient delusion, then a fixed idea, then a chronic infirmity, finally a mild insanity), but by a sudden plunge into the most violent mania."

HENRY VAN DYKE
FISHERMAN'S LUCK, 1913

We touched on fly selection in chapter 4, but in this chapter I'm going to discuss the specific insects and forage that you're likely to encounter on trout waters. Knowing a bit more of the life cycles of these insects will enable you to anticipate which bugs in which life stage the trout might be finding, and where. Knowing that trout are opportunistic predators and will consume nearly anything that lands on or swims in the water, we can entice them with a broader array of flies that imitate all these food items.

THE FOODS TROUT EAT

Most of the time, fly fishers use artificial flies that imitate insects, not larger forage, because trout eat so many insects. To gain a day's worth of calories a trout could eat one big shiner, and probably would if the opportunity were there every day. But it usually isn't. The opportunity to eat insects *does* occur regularly every day, however, especially when water temperatures favor both trout and aquatic insect activity, which happily (for the trout and us) happen to coincide.

Of the insects trout eat, the three major groups that live in the water are mayflies, caddisflies, and stoneflies. Trout see and feed on these insects the majority of the time. As you delve deeper into the species in each of these insect orders, you may find it convenient to use their Latin scientific order names: *Ephemeroptera*, *Trichoptera*, and *Plecoptera*, respectively. But I'll stick with their more common names here.

Many other insects that trout recognize as food are land-born terrestrials that often find themselves unintentionally falling or being blown into the water. Ants, leafhoppers, inchworms, grasshoppers, crickets, beetles, and many others can find themselves at the mercy of the water and trout. Most often these insects are available at the height of their abundance and activity, which is often at the height of summer, after the abundance of aquatic insects has waned. (Their imitations carry the same names.)

In still waters, while there are some mayflies and caddisflies, there are also special-

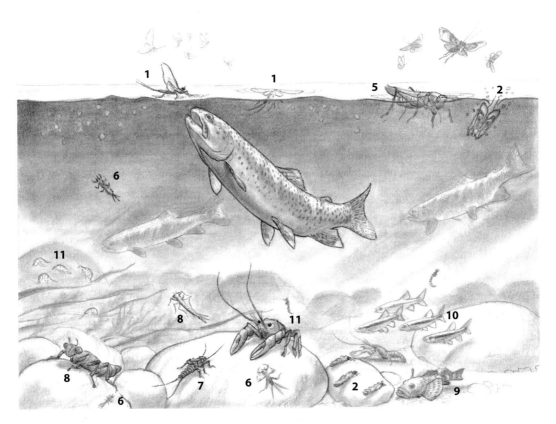

Food items from a trout's smorgasbord. Although air-breathing organisms are available to trout only at tightly defined times of the year, enough varieties of insects (mainly adults) come along to keep trout looking up for easy meals throughout the year. Underwater, most of these food items are available most of the year:

1. Mayfly duns and spinners are easy meals because, for different reasons, both are helpless on the surface of the water. Although there are over seven hundred species of mayflies, water fertility, purity, and temperature will dictate which species hatch on which waters (flowing and still) and for how long.

2. Caddisflies are often the most important insects in flowing waters. They occupy broader spectra of water

ized still-water insects such as mosquitoes and midges on which trout can focus. And there are predatory insects in still waters that offer bigger mouthfuls to trout, specifically the underwater life forms of dragonflies and damselflies. (Again, the imitations carry the same names—Mosquito Larva, Midge, Damselfly Nymph, etc.)

Trout also find crustaceans to be abundant and available in certain highly fertile waters. These include crayfish, those miniature imitations of lobsters that trout will certainly eat if they can find them. But much more abundant and available to trout are

temperature and fertility than mayflies and stoneflies, live longer as adults, and—with hundreds of species—are available to trout throughout the year.

3. Stoneflies (not shown) require pure, highly oxygenated, flowing water. Their nymphs are more important than their adult stage, although egg-laying adults over and on the water are relished by trout because of their large size.

4. Damselflies (not shown) are backwater or still-water insects. In their adult form, they're rarely available to trout, except when adult male damselflies pounce on newly emerging nymphs on the surface. Big trout will cruise in search of clusters of these adults.

5. Grasshoppers, along with a large array of other terrestrials, can be important trout food on moving or still water, especially when mature insects inadvertently fall, fly, or are blown into the water.

6. Mayfly nymphs become especially important to trout as they reach maturity and for a week or two before they hatch. Fortunately, enough species exist to keep mature nymphs available from early spring to late autumn.

7. Stonefly nymphs are exceptionally attractive food items because they often grow very large over the three to four years they need to mature. They're always available to trout, but only in the pure, cold, flowing waters they require to survive.

8. Dragonfly and damselfly nymphs survive and thrive in nearly any still-water environment. Where those waters also support trout, the trout will pursue these big, meaty nymphs with relish.

9. Trout waters also support many kinds of feed fish, including young trout fry (trout are cannibalistic), dace, madtoms, shiners, suckers, flatheads, sculpins (shown here), and others. Whenever they can, trout will eat these big mouthfuls.

10. Smelt are a cold-water-loving feed fish that inhabit many trout waters. Schooling fish, they're usually found in still water but migrate into moving water in the spring to spawn. Where smelt exist, trout and salmon pursue them relentlessly.

11. Crustaceans are often overlooked as trout food that can be imitated with flies, but trout will feast on crawfish, scuds, and cressbugs (sowbugs) because they often exist in large numbers.

Note: Many artificial flies are named to describe the organism they imitate—the Golden Stonefly Nymph, the Black-Nosed Dace, Joe's Smelt, the Yellowstone Scud, the West Branch Caddis, the Blue-Winged Olive Dun, the Pale Morning Dun, etc. Unfortunately, this rule does not always hold true. A Cahill imitates a mayfly, and a Stimulator, an adult stonefly. Knowing how food items look always helps in picking artificial flies to imitate them—mayfly wings are upright, caddisfly wings look like little pup tents, and so on. Matching the profile, size, and color of the artificial to the natural assures good fly selection.

the smaller freshwater shrimp—most often called *scuds*, as are their imitations—that can live in both moving and still water. They generally range from ⅛ to ¾ inch long. Where they occur, they're often available en masse, and often you're alerted to their abundance by finding them crawling all over your waders when you exit the water. The other major crustacean that trout will eat is called a cressbug (or sowbug), which looks like an enlarged flea and which, again, can be available in abundance.

Where they do occur, and where trout can find them, forage fish will be eaten with relish. If we can accurately imitate their form and color, we'll find trout anxious to take them. We'll come back to forage fish later in the chapter.

Are there other foods trout focus on? Yes, many, but often they're localized, like the runs of young lamprey eels in many Great Lakes streams. Remain observant and learn what trout are finding for food, then imitate that food and present the imitation in a realistic way.

MAYFLIES

The brief discussion of mayfly hatches in chapter 4 focused on one significant moment in the life of a mayfly, specifically that moment when it emerges from its underwater nymph phase and becomes an air-breathing adult. The mayfly life cycle includes four distinct phases in all, however, starting with eggs, which are the only phase that is not important to trout. The eggs are just too tiny to be of any food value. The entire cycle takes one year for most mayfly species (a few take two years, and fewer still take three).

Quickly—within about two weeks of their being deposited in the water—tiny mayfly eggs hatch into nymphs, the underwater phase of the life cycle, and as the nymphs grow they become increasingly important to trout. With only a year to mature into full-sized adult insects, these nymphs will shed their exoskeletons, called *chitin*, between twenty and thirty times. To do this, the nymph splits the chitin along its head and its back and steps out of the old skin. It must cling to some underwater vegetation and wait for its new exoskeleton to harden, a five- to ten-minute process that leaves it vulnerable to trout, out in the open as it is. (Here, use all-purpose nymph imitations like a Hare's Ear or a Pheasant Tail, unless you know the specific nymph and can imitate it.)

When it reaches maturity, the nymph migrates through the stream to a place that will provide its best chance for successfully swimming to the surface and emerging as an adult, known as a *dun*—that helpless critter that trout and anglers prize. This migration and subsequent rise to the surface prompts focused subsurface feeding from trout.

Of further importance is that the process of transforming from nymph to dun is what is known as an *emergence*. The nymph attaches itself to the bottom of the *menis-*

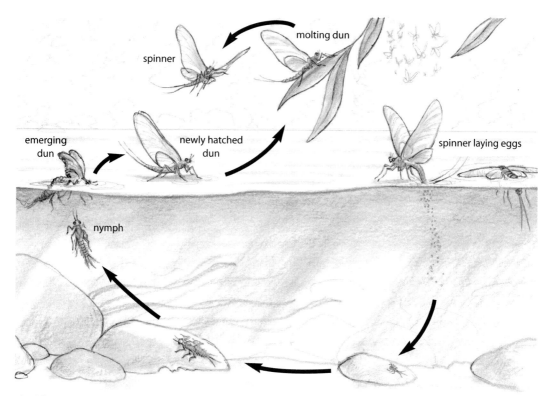

The life cycle of a mayfly begins with an adult (spinner) laying eggs. Quickly—within a week or two—the eggs hatch into tiny nymphs. During the next fifty weeks, the nymphs feed and grow, shedding their exoskeletons as they outgrow them up to thirty-five times. This helps explain why nymphs are always attractive to trout. Above the water, after emerging, a mayfly rarely lives more than twenty-four hours, completing one last molt from dun to spinner, mating, laying eggs, and dying. Different mayfly species (there are seven hundred of them) begin this cycle at different times of the year, from late winter through late autumn. The names of the phases—nymph, emerger, dun, spinner—are often incorporated into the names of the flies that imitate those phases: Pheasant Tail Nymph, Hendrickson Emerger, Iron Blue Dun, Trico Spinner.

cus, as that mystical membrane between water and air is known, and once again splits its chitin. Only this time, a mature dun emerges, not a larger form of the nymph. This is an especially difficult time for the insect, when it's not quite nymph and not quite dun, and trout will feed on these emergers with the same zeal they'll bring to the duns, and for the same reason—once attached to the meniscus, the emergers can't go anywhere. They're stuck there until they successfully become duns or die in the effort, as many do. Emerger patterns of artificial flies can be very effective at this time.

After they emerge from their chitin this last time, the duns must stand on the surface film until their wings are totally unfurled and dry in the air; then they lift off the water, generally flying up and across the stream to shoreside bushes and cover. In scientific parlance, these duns are known as *sub-imagoes*. (Here, your imitation reverts to the size, profile, and color formula.)

There is yet one more transformation left. Within one to two days, these duns will metamorphose into their final, sexually mature state, known as the *spinner* phase to anglers and *imagoes* to scientists. These spinners, when they're ready, then fly back out over the water, the males forming swarms into which the females will fly to select partners. They mate, and then the females fly off to deposit their eggs; some just drop them from the air, a few land flat on the water to do this, and fewer still actually submerge before releasing the eggs.

The mating process ends the same way for both males and females, with the *spinner fall*: the insects die over or on the water and their bodies float along, wings splayed, offering yet another meal to the trout. There are many splayed-wing artificial flies to imitate the individuals of a spinner fall, but you should certainly carry a small black spinner (aka a Trico), a Rusty Spinner, and a Mahogany Spinner, and fishing them nicely extends the time when trout will continue to rise to our flies.

This entire cycle—egg, nymph, dun, and spinner—is considered an incomplete metamorphosis; a complete cycle is the egg–larva–pupa–adult cycle we'll discuss with caddisflies. This incomplete cycle is similar to what we'll see for stoneflies later in this chapter.

It's also important to note that when we say mayflies have one-year life cycles— and sometimes two or three years depending on the species—we're talking fairly precisely. While hatches and emergences might be delayed or hurried a day or two because of weather or water temperatures, mayflies will hatch each year in the same order, with one species maintaining its temporal position relative to the others that flank it, and usually they'll hatch at the same time each year on a given water.

This fact helps us predict which mayfly we're likely to encounter depending on when we can get onto the stream. If we've already seen the mayflies known as Quill

Mayfly spinner imitations may have a variety of body colors, and their sizes may vary as they approximate the size of the natural spinner, but they all share the characteristics of having splayed, sparse wings, split tails to help them float, and no hackle. The Trico *(pictured here)* and Blue-Winged Olive are common spinner patterns. *(Orvis)*

Gordons, we know that the Hendricksons are due next, to be followed by the March Browns (in the East), and so on right through the year. This is not to say that we might not be seeing hatches of several species of mayflies at one time, but if we do see a multiple hatch this year, we'll probably encounter the same group of mayflies the next year at that same time, too.

Another important fact is that regional and area differences in hatches can occur, too, depending upon water quality, seasonal temperature variations, altitudes, and distances—hatches in the West are different from hatches in the East. Wherever trout and mayflies do occur, however, their relation is ancient and regular, and nowadays well documented.

Knowing when specific mayflies are due to hatch is obviously a huge aid in deciding which flies to carry and use. Nearly as important, however, is where on a stream they're likely to emerge. Remember that streams vary considerably from segment to segment, with riffles and rapids here, runs and pools there. Over the millions of years that mayflies have evolved, part of that evolution has been adapting to specific water types in nymph form. Knowing which waters nymphs prefer will help us predict not only where our nymph patterns will be most effective but also where on the river the hatch is likely to occur.

As detailed by Al Caucci and Bob Nastasi in their seminal work *Hatches*, there are four basic types of mayfly nymphs, classified by how their bodies have evolved to deal with different types of water: crawlers, clingers, swimmers, and burrowers. As you might imagine, these labels will help you pinpoint where these nymphs will be found. *Crawlers* prefer slow- to medium-flowing water, and they move about by walking along the streambed. *Clingers* have powerful legs and flattened bodies for maintaining their positions in the hard flows of rapids. *Swimmers* are slim and graceful and prefer gentle currents with backwaters and pockets. And *burrowers* need the soft bottom of large pools or still waters so that they can dig down into the mud and create burrows. (See illustration next page.)

The connection between nymph types and where their duns will emerge is significant. Crawler nymphs, for instance, include Hendricksons and Pale Morning and Evening Duns, whose adults emerge on slow- to medium-flowing water. Clingers produce Cahills and March Browns, which hatch in and below hard flows. Swimmers produce both small Blue-Winged Olives and larger Mahogany Duns, whose duns emerge in slower water. And burrowers often produce the huge mayflies like Green, Brown, and Gray Drakes that show up in slow backwaters or lakes and ponds.

These common names for mayflies will become more and more familiar to you as you inquire of anglers and at fly fishing stores which flies to use at what times of year.

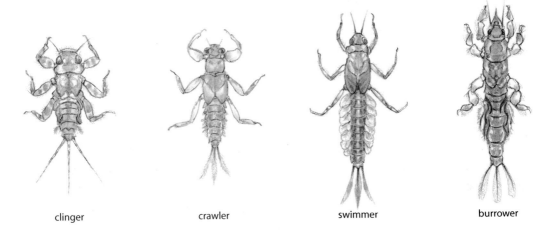

clinger   crawler   swimmer   burrower

Mayflies are often grouped according to their nymphal mode of life: clingers, crawlers, swimmers, and burrowers. Within all these groups the size of the nymph is highly variable as it develops through its many *instars* (the growing time between moltings).

Clingers inhabit swift water, are flattened and stocky, and always have their eyes on top of their heads. They belong to the family Heptageniidae, whose species include what are commonly referred to as March Browns, Gray Foxes, Light Cahills, Quill Gordons, and others.

Crawlers like moderate currents, can be very small to large at maturity, and always have their eyes on the sides of their heads. They comprise five families: Ephemerellidae (including Hendricksons, Sulfurs, Pale Evening Duns, Pale Morning Duns, and others); Leptophlebiidae (Iron Blue Duns and others); Leptohyphidae (represented by Tricos, among others); Caenidae (White-Winged Sulfurs); and Baetiscidae (rare).

Swimmers have slender, sleek bodies; long, fragile legs; and tails with hair fringes that are used for paddling. There are two important families: Baetidae (represented by Blue-Winged Olives) and Siphlonoridae (typically the Lead Wing Coachman).

Burrowers dig into the rich silts of backwaters and still waters. They are large nymphs at maturity, some reaching 1½ inches in length, with tusks on their mandibles, spadelike heads for digging, and serpentine bodies. Three families are important to anglers: Ephemeridae (with species commonly known as Green Drake, Yellow Drake, Brown Drake, and Hexagenia), Potamanthidae (including the Golden Drake), and Polymitarcyidae (including the White Fly).

And as you fish more and more, the questions you develop regarding the specific mayflies you're encountering will prompt you to ask more pointed questions and seek authoritative answers. It's beyond the scope of this book to carry the discussion of mayflies into much more detail. There are, however, any number of expert and accurate reference books available, and I've listed a selection of them in the bibliography.

CADDISFLIES

Caddisflies are often the most important insects trout eat. Trout are opportunistic feeders, and where caddisflies are abundant trout may focus on them almost exclusively.

And caddisflies are extremely abundant in a broad array of trout streams. Yet caddisflies are often the most frustrating insect to imitate accurately, and they offer special problems in the effective presentation of an appropriate artificial fly to trout.

Among the primary reasons for this frustration is that in caddisfly hatches, it's difficult to tell just what the trout are rising to. We'll see plenty of strong and splashy rises from trout, and we'll see plenty of caddisfly adults flitting and bouncing along on the surface of a stream. We can and do easily catch the pup tent–winged adults in streamside bushes and then easily match their profile, size, and color with an artificial, just as we do so successfully with mayfly duns. Then we'll fish the appropriate dry fly with increasing frustration as rising trout continue to ignore our precise offerings.

Yet in truth, the adult phase of a caddisfly isn't an easy target for a trout to catch. Indeed, it's the least sought after phase of the insect's entire life cycle, and you can understand why. *You* try to catch one of those skittering, bouncing, dapping adults out over the water. It's very difficult for you and for the trout. Yet there are the trout, rising regularly as we watch the adult caddisflies. What's going on here?

Unraveling this mystery involves understanding the life cycle of caddisflies, which in turn reveals where and when trout find their easiest meals.

As we said earlier, caddisflies mature through a complete metamorphosis that includes egg, larva, pupa, and adult; again, the eggs are of no consequence to the trout. This time, the wormlike larvae are the life forms that live and grow underwater, yet they have defenses that no mayfly nymph ever thought of. Many species of caddisfly larvae, though not all of them, create small shelters, called *cases*, in which to live (see art next page). They are often elaborate-looking abodes made from pebbles, twigs, or other ma-

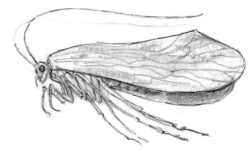

Adult caddisflies are meant to fly, and they do it well. Much of what we see when they're at rest is their wings, four of them, and they flit and dance and skitter across and above the water, making them difficult targets for trout. They range in size from 5 to 30 millimeters, or hook sizes 22 to 4.

terials and glued together with sticky silk that the larvae generate from their mouths. Specific species of caddis will build unique cases: some from grains of sand, some from slivers of wood; some round and long, others square and squat.

The cases are anchored to underwater vegetation or rocks and are easy to pick out and identify. They offer their inhabitants both a place from which to feed—the little larvae just stick their heads out to strain plankton from the current—and a place of

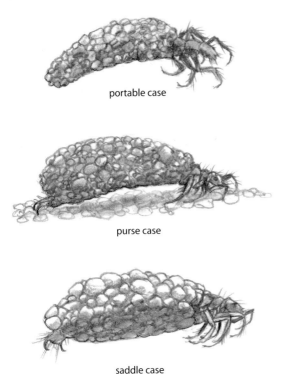

portable case

purse case

saddle case

Most caddis larvae build homes, called *cases*, from materials that are readily available. A few are free-living, and others hide down in the rocks and build food-catching nets. Case builders outgrow their homes a number of times and must rebuild them, sealing off the entrances only when they are mature and pupate. The free roamers and net builders build only one case in which they pupate. Shown here are saddle cases of the Black Caddis.

safety. Trout and other predators will rarely dislodge them from their cases. The larvae, however, are vulnerable when they outgrow their homes and must leave and build new ones, which occurs about five times before they mature. Often you can see trout with their noses on the rocks feeding on these homeless larvae. And it's then that a green or orange Caddisfly Larva, as it's called, will work well.

Other caddisfly larvae—some of the most important ones for trout and anglers—live without cases, instead building underwater nets that help them seine plankton. And still other larvae are free-swimming, often using their silk to hold their bodies in the current, using the silk as a lifeline, or lengthening it to rappel downstream. The net-builders and free-swimming caddis larvae are vulnerable to trout predation, but they use the cover of the streambed effectively for protection. The same larvae artificials as above imitate these larvae, too.

When trout are feeding on larvae, the most important natural occurrence for a trout and an angler is the dispersal behavior of the caddis larvae. In the evening, just after dusk, many of these larvae, both the cased species and the free-swimmers, will rise into the water column and drift along for some time in search of new sections of the stream. Scientists think that this action, called *behavioral drift*, is meant to disperse the insects along broad reaches of streams. Free-drifting imitations of the larvae at this time, and again just before dawn, can provide excellent angling action.

The larvae feed and grow and move around to new sections of stream and to new cases through much of the year. But when they're just reaching maturity, they use their silk to seal off their existing cases or, if the larvae are free-living, to build and seal off their first cases. Then they pupate.

Pupation is the process by which many insects change from worms to winged adults. Butterflies are the most visible example. For caddisflies, pupation takes place underwater and out of sight. When the metamorphosis from the larval worm to the adult is complete, the caddisfly cuts through the opening of its case and, still surrounded by its pupal shuck, swims and drifts to the surface of the stream. Many of these shuck-encased adults drift along just below the meniscus, while many others actually attach to the bottom of the meniscus. In either case they are vulnerable as they struggle to escape the pupal shuck, and this is when trout attack them.

Because of pupation, adult caddisflies are fully formed and ready to fly off once they escape their pupal shucks. Trout have plenty of experience with this and are instinctively aware that a struggling insect at the surface can quickly escape, ergo the slashing and showy rises. The trout are not usually trying to target and catch adults, but they do know that if they aren't quick, their easy meal can escape. Too often we anglers are left thinking that trout are targeting the adults we're seeing all over the water when they're actually after the pupal emergers.

As with emerging mayfly nymphs, fishing emerging caddisfly pupal imitations just below the surface or right in it is usually our most effective tactic. Yet also like mayfly nymphs, many caddis adults can't escape their pupal shucks. That's when an emerger pattern with a trailing shuck or an adult imitation with a trailing shuck can be particularly effective. It's also why just enough trout will take our dead-drifted adult imitations to make us think they're targeting adults even when they're after the emerging pupae.

Once free of their shucks, the adult caddisflies usually take a hop or two on the surface and fly off to streambank bushes. Unlike mayflies, these adults are sexually mature now and need no further transformation, and they'll live for several days to several months, drinking nectar or water to sustain themselves. (Mayfly spinners have no mouth parts and rarely live more than twenty-four hours.)

Caddisflies breed in the streamside brush. The females return to the water to deposit their eggs. Although a few species drop their eggs above the water and some others attach them to branches, logs, or bridges from which the hatching larvae will drop into the water, the great majority lay their eggs directly on, or more often down in, the water. Both these latter behaviors are important for anglers because they leave the females vulnerable to trout.

When females lay eggs on the water, they'll often dip their abdomens into the water or actually splay their wings and bodies onto the water to release their eggs. The effort often leaves them resting or trapped on the meniscus, where they may drift over feeding fish. And although they're capable of breeding and laying eggs up to four or five times, eventually they'll die, usually on or in the water. (Here an Elk Hair Caddis of appropriate size and color will work well when drifted drag-free.)

The caddisfly's most common means of laying eggs is by literally carrying them down into the water either by walking from the shore or diving directly into the water. The wings of the adult insects are covered with tiny hairs that trap air, and these entrained air bubbles will sustain the female for up to an hour as she attaches long strings of eggs to streambed rocks and rubble. The females then drift and swim back to the surface, again escape the meniscus, and fly off. It's during this egg-laying activity, either when the females are swimming down to the bottom or especially when they're returning to the surface, that manipulating an artificial fly, usually a wet fly like a Cahill, Brown Hackle, or Partridge and Green, can be very productive (see chapter 8).

To recap, caddisflies are abundant and important to trout. Larval imitations are most productive just after dusk and before daylight during behavioral drift. Hatches of caddisflies are best imitated with emerging pupal artificials, not adult imitations. And the most productive patterns for imitating egg-laying females are wet flies. Are adult imitations ever effective? Yes, but more during egg-laying activities or with added attached pupal shucks. Again, a number of informative and detailed books are listed in the bibliography.

STONEFLIES

Stoneflies are important as trout food because they live in particularly cold, pure, well-oxygenated water, as do trout, and because they often grow to very large sizes. Rarely will a trout pass up a meal of a big stonefly nymph, and indeed the trout will often move some distance to capture it. Where stoneflies occur, imitating them can be the best method for anglers to attract any trout, including the biggest trout in the stream.

Stonefly imitations are not effective, however, on all trout waters. Because of their primitive array of gill filaments, stoneflies need pure, cold water that has a high percentage of dissolved oxygen. They won't be found in streams that are slow moving, or tend to warm in the summer, or receive silty runoff water in the spring. Any of these factors would suffocate stoneflies and extirpate them. Streams higher up in the hills and mountains that stay cold and have ample sections of rapids are stonefly heavens. Although stoneflies are particularly famous in the West, they occur across the continent, East and West.

The stonefly life cycle is similar to that of mayflies except that stoneflies do not undergo a spinner metamorphosis, instead following the egg, nymph, adult life cycle. In addition, their nymph phase can last two to four years, depending on the species, and because the nymphs live so long underwater, one generation or another is always approaching full size, making them constantly attractive to trout.

Because they crawl out of the water before splitting their nymphal cases and emerging as adults, the nymphal shucks of stoneflies are often obvious on bushes, trees, and buildings near streams where they live. Look for them to give you hints about what size and color of nymph imitation to tie on.

When the nymphs do mature, some rise and hatch onto the surface, where trout will feed on them. These surface-hatching stoneflies generally occur early in the season. Most often, however, stonefly nymphs that are nearing their hatching time crawl out of the water onto some rock or bush, where their chitin dries and splits and the adult steps out. This type of hatching, of course, makes the adults unavailable to trout. You can identify stonefly adults by the way they carry their wings flat against their backs when they're at rest (versus upright for mayflies and like a pup tent for caddisflies).

Breeding takes place in streamside bushes, then the females either walk onto the water or fly out over it before plopping down to release their eggs. The adults can live for up to a month, but ten days to two weeks is more common, with the females returning to the water to deposit eggs several times. Each time the females are on the water, they're susceptible to trout and attractive because of their size. Eventually, the females will finish with egg laying and lie exhausted and dying on the water surface. That's when they provide the easiest meals for trout.

Fishing stonefly imitations, then, is a matter of imitating the nymph much of the time, and then enjoying the brief time when adults are available. You still need to choose a fly that mimics the natural, however, because stoneflies cover a broad spectrum of colors and sizes. This rule of thumb will help: Early-season stoneflies are smaller and dark, often black, and usually emerge on the water; late-spring and early-summer stoneflies are the largest of the year, and generally emerge on land; late-summer and autumn stoneflies are the lighter-colored species, and they also emerge on land.

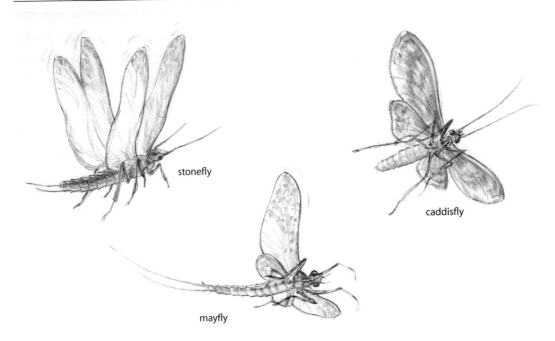

stonefly

caddisfly

mayfly

Mayflies, caddisflies, and stoneflies all range from ¼ inch to more than 1½ inches long, so size alone won't help in identification, particularly in flight. A quick glance at the way an insect is flying, along with some obvious details, however, will tell you which insect you're observing.

Stoneflies in flight have four obvious wings that flap only above their bodies, never below. They often look like miniature, overburdened helicopters.

Caddisflies are mothlike, with four strong wings that beat both above and below the body. They're agile fliers and flit, dive, and soar.

Mayfly duns fly with difficulty and not far. When they lift off the water, they generally fly directly to shoreside cover. Mayfly spinners, however, do fly well and often form swarms of males over the water that females enter to find mates. Both as duns and spinners, mayflies beat their wings, of which only two are prominent, above and below their bodies.

Stonefly hatches in the West—particularly the famous salmonfly hatch and the golden stonefly hatch—are exciting, much anticipated events. Big, cumbersome stoneflies whirlygig their way up into the air in such numbers that you may think a plague of locusts of biblical proportions has erupted. The insects, which may be 2 inches long, fly poorly and splat against windshields and on roadways, while trout feast and gorge out in the stream. This abundance sweeps upstream for several days in a wave of insect activity, and veteran anglers will follow its progress upstream, too. Identifying adult flying stoneflies is easy because they look so cumbersome and because, when airborne, they beat their wings only above their bodies. Mayflies, caddisflies, and locusts have a full wing-beat that travels both above and below their bodies.

While stonefly nymph patterns work well all year long, they are especially effective when the nymphs begin their migration toward the shore. Then the nymphs are out of their hiding spots in the rock rubble of the streambed, making them much more available to trout. As always, you need to know the size and color of the natural you're imitating.

Fishing stonefly imitations is something of a way of life in the West. The insects are so big and abundant that they're impossible to ignore. But in the East, few anglers are aware of their importance. This is mainly because Eastern stoneflies rarely emerge in the vast numbers of their Western counterparts, and even when they do emerge in numbers, the emergence is often after dark. Still, stoneflies are available to Easterners and their trout, and many veteran fly fishers guard their use of stonefly imitations as if they alone had discovered a mysterious and mystical method for catching big trout.

Because stoneflies need pristine waters to thrive and therefore are not as widespread as other aquatic insects, the literature for them is not as extensive as that for mayflies and caddisflies. Still, I've listed some excellent books in the bibliography.

Stonefly imitations can range in size from the 2-inch-long Giant Black Stonefly on the far left to the tiny $^3/_8$-inch Brassie on the far right. Between these two, *(left to right)*, are a second version of the Giant Black Stonefly, a Golden Stonefly, a Brown Stone, a Montana, two Hare's Ears tied on long shank hooks, and a Brown Larva Lace.

COMPARATIVE SEASONAL ABUNDANCES OF INVERTEBRATE TROUT FORAGE

The graph shows the relative availabilities to trout of mayflies, caddisflies, stoneflies, and terrestrial insects as the seasons progress on and in a typical stream. The graph is generalized, ignoring such unique characteristics of individual streams as a superabundance of one kind of forage or the relative scarcity of another. Yet this depiction holds true as a widespread and long-term average and gives an idea of which insects you should be looking for when and at what water temperatures. (Broadly speaking—and we *are* speaking broadly here—these seasonal abundance patterns for mayflies, caddisflies, and terrestrials apply on still water as well.)

Mayflies are, for anglers, the most imitated and appreciated aquatic trout food for two reasons. First, when they hatch, the dun (sub-imago) stands on the surface of the water unfurling and drying its wings, helpless to escape trout predation. Trout will focus on mayfly duns exclusively when they're available. Second, mayflies emerge in an orderly and predictable fashion each year on each stream where they occur. If the Quill Gordons have already hatched, the Hendricksons are next, then the March Browns, and so on. The species of mayflies on each stream may vary, but the order of their emergence won't, and that order will become reassuringly familiar to you over time on your favorite streams. That said, it's important to note that these hatches will overlap, with the end of the Quill Gordon hatching period often trailing into the beginning of the Hendrickson hatch, and so on, and trout may be focused on one or the other dun.

Caddisflies also have a peak hatching period. They may well be more important than mayflies, both because they are more numerous than mayflies on the trout waters where they coexist and because they thrive in waters that, for one reason or another, do not support mayflies. Generally, they too emerge

GENERAL AVAILABILITY AND ABUNDANCE OF INVERTEBRATES

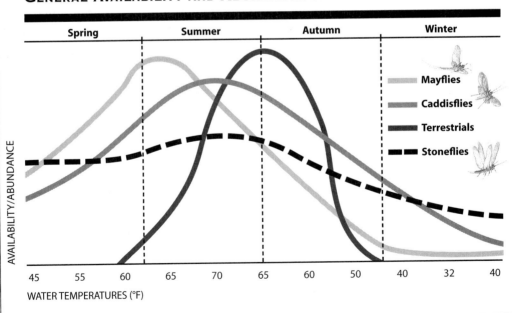

in a regular order, but because the adults live longer than mayfly duns and because some caddisflies have more than one generation per year, this orderly emergence blurs.

Stoneflies have a much flatter abundance curve than either mayflies or caddisflies because their life cycle is much longer, with their nymphs living underwater two to four years. In addition, the majority of stoneflies crawl out of the water to hatch, making them unavailable to trout at this time. Only when the females return to the water to lay eggs are dry flies productive. One other factor is important with stoneflies. They require pure, cold, well-oxygenated water to live. Marginal or even average trout streams may have no stoneflies in them at all, which is why their abundance curve is lower than the curves of other invertebrates, and stoneflies are rare in still water except when deposited there by feeder streams. Where they do occur, however, they are big, meaty mouthfuls, and trout will take them whenever they can.

Terrestrial insects are underappreciated. When a flying ant swarm is inadvertently hitting the water, trout will feast on them. When there's an abundance of grasshoppers, as often happens in the West, you'll see even sated trout gulping them down. Terrestrials are, however, inconsistent in their availability. You need to see them on the water and then match them with the appropriate fly.

Forage fish are not graphed here because they're available to trout year-round in relatively stable numbers. Where they're abundant, they'll form an important part of a trout's diet throughout the year. Yet even then, trout will often focus on the easier to catch insects when they're available.

TERRESTRIALS

Terrestrial insects and their imitations have long been important to trout and to anglers. As long ago as the sixteenth century, when the first dozen artificial flies were described by Dame Juliana Berners in her famous *Treatyse of Fysshynge wyth an Angle*, two of the twelve patterns were terrestrials. Since then, many angling writers have turned their eyes and pens toward terrestrials, but none with more acute observation than Vincent Marinaro in his book, *A Modern Dry-Fly Code*.

What these angling writers tell us is that although aquatic insects are certainly important, terrestrial insects can garner the focused attention of trout anytime they're available, even when emerging aquatics are present. Aquatic insects are designed to rise to the surface and then fly away. When terrestrials are on or in the water, however, it's by accident. They fall out of the bushes or trees or are blown into the water, or simply march into the water like lemmings. Once there, terrestrials are in a foreign environment and are helpless. They aren't designed to swim, and they can't fly away. Trout are quick to identify a helpless, easy meal that takes little effort (or energy) to capture.

When larger terrestrials are in the water and fish are rising to them, it's not difficult to decide which pattern to select. If a hot wind in July is blowing big grasshoppers into the water, our big hopper pattern is perfect. Ditto the swarms of big male flying ants that can carpet a trout stream.

When terrestrials are available, usually from the height of summer through early autumn, they can form the majority of a trout's diet. A good selection of terrestrials would include *(left to right)* a Jassid (imitating a leafhopper), an Ant, a Ladybug, an Inchworm, a larger Ant, and a Grasshopper.

What Marinaro discovered, however, was the importance and indeed the preeminence of small, even tiny terrestrials: ants, leafhoppers, and beetles. Rises from trout to no visible insect prompted Marinaro to investigate, and he discovered not only the abundance of these minute morsels but also how they sit low in and even under the meniscus. He developed the Jassid dry fly to imitate leafhoppers and the Double Jassid, or Beetle, to imitate beetles. In designing his flies, he realized that trout focus on the silhouette of an insect and the way the insect refracts the light trout see below the surface. This information allowed him to use weightless feathers and hooks on his tiny flies—some down to size 22—and to effect the reconstruction of many other standard dry flies. His contributions have been invaluable.

Nowadays we have not only Berners's and Marinaro's observations, plus those of many other close observers and innovators, but also plenty of new materials with which terrestrial imitations are constructed. Closed-cell foam makes superb ant imitations, and new, simple constructions such as the Madam X and the Humpy are easy to tie and effective. What we must bring individually to the trout stream is, again, our close observation of what the trout are finding for food. It's one thing to know that tiny terrestrials constitute an important source of nutrition for trout. It's quite another to actually identify the terrestrials on any given day. Marinaro used a scrap of cheesecloth hung between two sticks to seine out and identify the minute terrestrials that were so baffling. You can do the same, or you can buy pocket-sized, fine-mesh fabric nets that are attached between two small poles. Yes, it's another widget, but mine has saved my day many times.

STILL-WATER FOODS

What you've learned about identifying and imitating aquatic insects in flowing water will serve you well in still waters, too. Certain species of caddisflies and mayflies inhabit, even prefer, still waters and provide exciting angling action there. Yet the abundance of both these insect orders pales in still water in the presence of true flies (Diptera).

True flies have two, not four, wings, and they include such familiar insects as deerflies, midges, mosquitoes, and blackflies. By some estimates their abundance as larvae can approach fifty thousand per square yard of lake bottom. Like caddisflies, Diptera develop through a complete metamorphosis and they're most susceptible as their pupal forms rise through the water and attach to the meniscus. It's equally important to anglers that because many Diptera have multiple generations per year, these flies are available all year long as important trout food. The trout see them and feed on them almost constantly by cruising just below the surface and inhaling rising pupae, emerging flies, and stillborn adults.

Effectively imitating the rising larvae and pupae is the best way to take advantage of these hatches of Diptera. It often means using surprisingly small, wormlike artificial flies, especially for the very important midges, fished on or right below the surface. These small flies—in the size 18 to 22 range—can and do catch astoundingly large trout. Some hatching Diptera are larger and cover a range of colors, so ask questions at the fly shop or seine some pupal samples when you suspect the trout are focused on Diptera.

Trout are not the only predators to appreciate this abundance of food. Two much larger insects gobble down nymphs, larvae, pupae, and adult flies, and they're instantly recognizable: damselflies, which hold their wings over their backs when at rest, and dragonflies, which hold their wings out to the sides.

In the air above the water, these agile, mature insects easily capture prey, yet it's as underwater nymphs that they interest anglers. There, they are as voracious as they are after maturing. They capture insects by zooming about like little attack submarines, gobbling down any living organism they can overwhelm—larvae, nymphs, or even small fry and shiners. And they grow large. These big mouthfuls of food, the dragon- and damselfly nymphs, bring fast strikes from cruising trout.

As mentioned at the beginning of this chapter, many other food items are available to trout, and they can be especially important in still waters. These include crustaceans, forage fish, leeches, and others. As in streams, the major determinants of which forage exist in which still waters vary from place to place. Water fertility, depth, temperature extremes, and purity as well as geographic location, acidity, and mineral con-

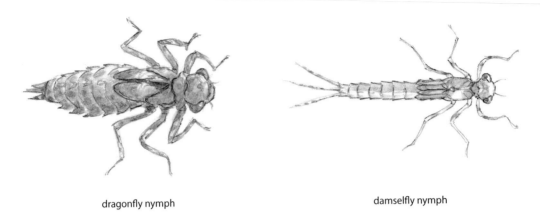

dragonfly nymph   damselfly nymph

Dragonfly nymphs are the bullies of still waters. They are large, up to 1½ inches long, chunky, and agile. These voracious predators scoot short distances with surprising speed. Damselfly nymphs are much more svelte, though no less ferocious. They'll sometimes reach 2 inches in length and also swim exceptionally well.

tent all affect which forage you might find trout focused on. Once again, careful observation and curiosity are invaluable.

FORAGE FISH

Without a doubt, big trout need big meals to survive. And biologists have proven that when big trout were smaller, they needed big meals to grow large. We also know that the majority of those big meals are provided by forage fish—the minnows, smelt, sculpins, and young trout that inhabit cold-water streams and lakes. By understanding which forage fish big trout are feeding on and how they are finding these feed fish, we can imitate these important food items and target the largest fish in a lake or stream.

Knowing the exact species of feed fish occurring in a particular water is not as important as it might be for insects. The differences among feed fish are subtle, and it often takes a trained taxonomist to identify them. (There are, for instance, over two thousand species of minnows.) Instead, the best advice for imitating feed fish with streamer flies is to observe the general shape, size, and color of the natural.

Dave Whitlock, in his *Guide to Aquatic Trout Foods*, has done us a great service by dividing feed fish into four categories: (1) deep-sided, thin-backed fish like alewives, shiners, smelt, and shad; (2) long, oval-bodied fish like chubs, dace, and trout; (3) compressed-bodied, wide-bellied fish like sculpins, madtoms, darters, and suckers; and (4) the eggs and newborn fry of trout and salmon. Classifying the feed fish we find in trout waters into one of these categories gives us the size and shape of

Streamer flies that cover most situations would include *(top row, from left)* the Mickey Finn, Black-Nosed Dace, Olive Woolly Bugger; and *(bottom row, from left)* Muddler Minnow, Joe's Smelt. Give them action that makes them stand out as injured or vulnerable, and big trout will be interested. *(Orvis)*

the imitation we need to use. Then, by observing the colors of the natural, we can imitate it fairly accurately. Whitlock's categories might be represented by the following imitations: (1) Joe's Smelt, (2) Black-Nosed Dace, (3) Muddler Minnow, and (4) Thunder Creek.

We can also decide how to fish these flies by understanding a few of their characteristics, as grouped by Whitlock. Category 1 feed fish—the alewives, smelt, shad, and shiners—are generally schooling fish and are most often found in still-water lakes, ponds, and impoundments. The trout will often cruise the fringes of these big schools, picking off individuals or chasing them to the surface to disorient them. Most of these species, but particularly smelt, stage at the mouths of inlet streams in the spring before spawning, and trout are never far away. Category 2 feed fish are happiest in much smaller groups or alone and generally prefer moving water. Category 3 fish are mostly bottom feeders in flowing water, are solitary, and depend upon camouflage for protection. Category 4 fish occur in the trout and salmon spawning areas of rivers and streams.

Of course there are tried-and-true imitations that are popular in particular areas, and a visit to the local tackle or bait shop can reveal the predominant feed fish via the streamer flies that are most prominent and popular. Here's a sampling to give you an idea of what to look for, based on Whitlock's categories: (1) Janssen Shad Minnow, Gray or Black Ghost, Joe's Smelt; (2) Black-Nosed Dace, Thunder Creek series, the Match-the-Minnow series, Golden Shiner; (3) Muddler Minnow, Dahlberg Diver,

Whitlock's Matuka Sculpin; and (4) Glo Bug, Egg-Sucking Leech, Alaska Salmon Smolt.

Armed with this information and with the basic presentation methods discussed in chapter 4, catching big trout with streamer flies should be a more enticing way to approach this underrated method of fly fishing.

Have we covered everything trout consume? No. But we've covered most of the food items that are predictable and regular in their occurrence. And this thumbnail sketch of food categories can form the basis of years, even lifetimes, of further study. You don't need to become fanatical about the study of trout foods, but you may find yourself as fascinated by these creatures as you are by trout themselves.

8 | Presenting Flies to Trout

"You want adrenaline? Try locating a 20-inch brown sipping ants three inches from the bank of a vodka-clear, slow-moving spring creek."

WILLIAM G. TAPPLY
"EXTREME ANGLING," IN GRAY'S SPORTING JOURNAL, FEBRUARY/MARCH 2003

The central problem in fly fishing is to get a fish to strike your fly. Fly selection is of premier importance in this, of course, especially when trout are focused on specific food items as discussed in the last chapter. Less obvious, however, is the importance of getting the fly to *act* like the natural food item it's supposed to be imitating.

Depending on the circumstances, trout will make a meal out of any of hundreds of food items, most of which not only look different but act different, too. When observing what trout are feeding on, therefore, we should also observe how that food item is acting. Does it float on the surface at the whim of the current, like a mayfly dun? Does it skitter along the surface or perhaps disappear from the surface altogether, like mature caddisflies? Do subadult aquatic insects crawl along the bottom or swim? Do crustaceans swim backward or forward? Do the feed fish depend upon camouflage for safety, staying close to the bottom, or on numbers for safety, schooling together?

The answers to these and other questions will help us decide *how* to present our flies. And because our only connection to the fly is through the fly line, the right casting strategies will present our flies in a more lifelike and enticing manner.

DRY FLY STRATEGIES

Heaven for a fly fisher is standing on the edge of a stream with a steady hatch of mayflies littering the surface and an array of trout slurping them down. Nirvana is having the right dry fly for that hatch on the end of your tippet. Everything that has come before this chapter is intended to put you in this situation. If you're like me, your eyes will get wide and your knees weak, and your first few casts will be as unsteady as a toddler trying to stand up for the first time.

But wait here a moment. Look closer, even straight down, at some drifting duns if you can. What you'll see are delicate insects standing up on their toes. You might see them trying and failing to get airborne, and you might see tiny concentric rings of

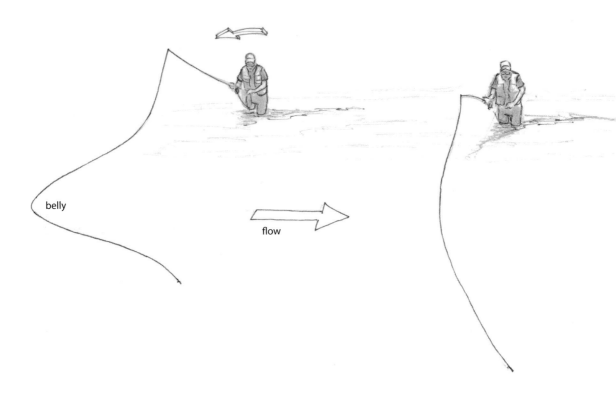

belly

flow

The mend cast is a useful tactic for putting an up- or downstream bow, or belly, in your line before it settles onto the water—when casting across swift water, for example. Do this by flicking your rod tip upstream (as here) or downstream as the line on the forecast straightens out in front of you.

ripples in the surface as they plop back down, but what you won't see is a V-shaped wake behind them.

When you start casting your perfect dry fly to these rising trout, it can't produce a V-shaped wake either, or the trout will see something unnatural. And unnatural to a trout means dangerous.

A V-shaped wake, or drag, is produced when some part of your line, leader, or tippet moves at a different speed—faster or slower—than your fly does and drags the fly along the surface. As mentioned in chapter 2, what you're trying to accomplish is a drag-free drift.

Your most advantageous cast to combat drag is upstream and across the current, but the vagaries and varieties of flowing water, and where the fish hold in that water, will often demand a more inventive response. The few possibilities discussed here will form the basis of your strategies; as your experience grows, adapt these approaches to the situations you encounter.

While the up-and-across cast is ideal for water flowing at a uniform speed, the most frequent problem on a stream is that tongues of intervening current will be moving faster or slower than the water in your target area. Certainly you can mend an upstream or downstream bow in your line after it has settled onto the water, but a better idea is to throw that mend into the line *before* the line is on the water. You make this *mend cast* by flicking the rod tip toward the upstream or downstream side after you have stopped it on the forecast (see illustration opposite). Make the flick immediately, and the mend will be farther toward the fly; a bit slower, and the mend will be closer to you. This is an especially effective tool when you have a well-delineated current to cross. Eventually you'll be able to put the bow in the line just where you need it, and it will give you a substantially longer drag-free drift.

Easier to accomplish but a bit less effective is the *reach cast*. Use it when you face the common problem of the center of the stream flowing uniformly faster or slower than your target area. When the current is faster, after you've stopped the rod tip on the forecast, reach upstream with your rod before the line has landed on the water, moving the rod tip in that direction, too. This will put the majority of the line upstream of your fly so that it must travel a greater distance than your fly. On those rare occasions when the current is slower between you and your target, make the same reaching motion downstream. Your fly in the faster-moving water will travel a greater distance, drag-free, to catch up with the slower-moving line.

When you have multiple currents to deal with, say in pocket water or on streams with many underwater boulders, you can put many little bends in your fly line, a tactic called the *slack cast*. Do this using one of two methods. The first is to wiggle the rod tip back and forth just after you've stopped it on the forecast. Like the mend cast

The reach cast, as shown here, is valuable where a hard-flowing current runs between you and your target area. This cast puts a mend in the line before the line hits the water. Then, by making quick secondary mends on the water, you'll increase the time that your fly is drifting naturally without drag.

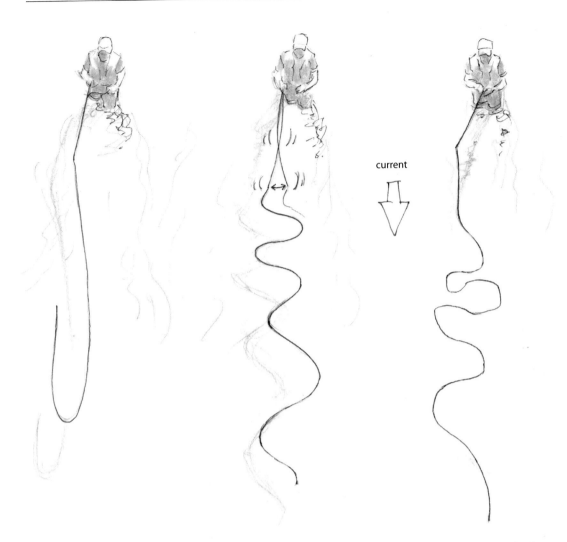

current

The slack cast is an exaggerated mend cast. Instead of flicking the rod tip once, you wiggle it back and forth as the line straightens on the forecast. This puts multiple S-shapes into the line, especially effective for presenting a fly directly downstream.

just described, the motion will put several smaller mends in the line so that when it lands on the water you'll see a series of little S-shapes, each of them combating drag.

You can accomplish the same thing by overpowering your forecast—casting a longer line than you need and casting it strongly. Be sure to aim upstream of your target so that the trout doesn't see your line, then stop your cast abruptly. The line and the fly will snap back toward you somewhat, effectively putting S-shapes into the line.

The methods just described will usually serve for crossing conflicting currents on

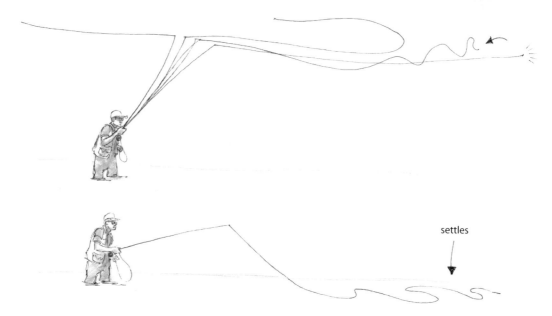

The slack cast may also be accomplished by overpowering the forecast. The fly line snaps back somewhat, creating the desired S-shapes. It's a bit tricky to accomplish at first, requiring just the right amount of extra power to produce the S-shaped loops.

a stream, but there are times when you'll need to cast to trout directly upstream or downstream from you. The reach cast is especially effective for an upstream lie because you can put the fly line to the side of a trout and have just the fly drift over him. You can use a slack or S-shaped cast for a trout directly downstream from you. If you didn't put the S-shapes into the line, the straight downstream flow of water would immediately drag your fly.

There are, in addition, several specialized presentations of dry flies that mimic the actions of their corresponding naturals. Although you won't use these presentations nearly as often as you do the drag-free drift, knowing they exist can help you focus on making your fly mimic the natural.

One of the most obvious of these is to make your fly plop down onto the water as a big terrestrial, like a grasshopper, would when accidentally falling into the water. You mimic this plop, which can draw the attention of trout from fairly long distances, by aiming your fly directly at the water surface instead of floating out the fly line just above the water as you normally would. You're attempting to get the fly to plop, but you don't want the fly line to hit hard, so aim your cast lower to the water than you normally would but not on the water. It helps to stop your backcast just before the rod tip reaches vertical, thus angling the backcast up higher behind you. Then your forecast angles downward, and the fly hits the water with a plop.

You can also use this method of casting to get your fly under overhanging obstacles on the bank—brush or tree limbs, for example. Because you're aiming the fly low, you can shoot it under the obstacle, which is particularly effective when leafhoppers, inchworms, or beetles are falling off the branches in question.

Certain flies, like soft-hackled flies tied to imitate emerging caddisflies, are best plopped onto the surface, too. Make that same strong, low cast toward your target area, and the plop of the fly drives it into the meniscus, where it will pick up a bubble of air. That bubble effectively imitates the bubbles that help caddisfly pupae swim to the surface, and the added sparkle of the air bubble can often get fussy trout to strike.

Certain naturals, such as some caddisflies and stoneflies and a few mayflies, do land on the surface of a stream to drop their eggs. In attempting to get airborne again, they can skitter along the surface and will occasionally leave short V-wakes like a dragged artificial. The key word here is "short." In their effort to escape the stream, they do skitter for short distances, and sometimes adding a skittering motion to your artificial can cause a quick strike. Just make sure your short skitter is followed by a short drag-free drift, because that's what the naturals will do.

Similarly, you can let your dry fly swing across the current at the end of its drag-free drift. Especially effective is when your dry fly, such as a caddisfly artificial, makes this swing just under the surface. To sink your fly, give a short tug on the line just as the fly begins to drag. The tug puts the fly just under the meniscus, where it imitates

To get a dry fly—particularly a big terrestrial like a hopper—to plop into the water and draw attention, you need the plane of your cast to angle up behind you and down toward your target area. Stopping your backcast before it reaches vertical will get your line to run along an upward incline behind you. On the forecast, make your stopping point lower, causing the line to angle downward. If your aim is accurate and your cast true, the fly will plop into its target area. This cast is also an effective way to shoot a fly under overhanging branches.

either a returning, egg-laying adult caddis or a drowned or emerging mayfly.

As mentioned in chapter 6, one fairly simple skill might be the most useful specialized tactic you employ in fishing dry flies as well as other fly types, and that is being able to cast with either hand. I'm right-handed, and although I certainly will never look like an accomplished fly caster with my left hand, I encounter a number of occasions each season when the only way to effectively present a fly near a streambank is to cast with my left hand. When I first tried it I was surprised how easily I could get a cast to roll out. After all, it's still your brain trying to get the line to do the same thing, just with your other hand.

Nymph Strategies

Fishing nymphs dramatically increases your productive time on the stream, and for much of that time, a good strike indicator (or dry fly) with a deep-running nymph will produce very well. This approach is the one to use when you can't see your quarry or you aren't sure a hatch is imminent, and I use it most of the time. But there are, in addition, several specialized strategies to use either side of a hatch—before or after it—and when you can actually see a fish. And there are a couple of others for special water conditions.

Before and after a hatch, you should imitate not only the specific insect that's hatching but also what the nymphs or pupae are doing.

As a mayfly hatch approaches, the nymphs will be testing their ability to rise to the surface. They'll literally be swimming up and down in the water column, where the trout will be looking for them. Making your artificial do the same thing will be highly effective because the trout have focused their attention off the bottom and are actively seeking these organisms. You can use your standard strike indicator and nymph rig, but your indicator may be out of the water some of the time, which is OK.

Use your usual up-and-across-the-stream cast, but raise your rod tip once the nymph has reached the bottom, effectively stopping the drag-free drift, and make your fly rise toward the surface. Your strike indicator will come out of the water, but you don't need it during this action because any strike of your rising fly will be felt on the straight line.

Before the nymph gets all the way to the surface, drop your rod tip back down and let the fly sink toward the bottom. Now your strike indicator does become important, for you've lost that direct connection to the artificial. If it twitches or moves at all unusually, set the hook. Continue this action as long as you can, then let the nymph swing across the current below you. Then pick up the line and do it again.

An adaptation of this method called the *Leisenring Lift* was developed in the 1940s by Jim Leisenring for tempting a fish you can see. In effect, you get the nymph to start its ascent just a foot in front of the fish, and rarely will that fish ignore such an easy meal. For this to work, you must be able to see the fish, you must be directly opposite the fish, and you must raise the nymph at the precise right moment. These conditions don't align often, and you need to get into position carefully because if you can see the fish, he can see you, too. But when the setup is there, this presentation is nearly ideal.

A similar strategy involves less movement on your part and doesn't demand that you be exactly opposite a fish. You still need to be able to see the fish, but this time you drift your nymph to the near side of the fish, and you watch the fish, not your indicator. As your nymph approaches the fish, see whether the fish curls toward it. If he does, set the hook, for rarely will a trout make that kind of effort without taking the fly. If the fish doesn't turn, let the fly pass some way below him and then recast, perhaps a bit closer to the fish but still on the near side.

Each of these strategies relegates the indicator to a role of lesser significance, and this is a good thing. Even though a strike indicator dramatically improves your rate of hookups when using nymphs, there's still a lag between when the fish picks up the nymph and when you see the indicator pause or move, and in that brief time the fish may recognize that your fly isn't food and may drop it. With these more specialized methods either you are watching the fish directly or you can feel the strike immediately; either way, you know much sooner that a fish has taken the fly.

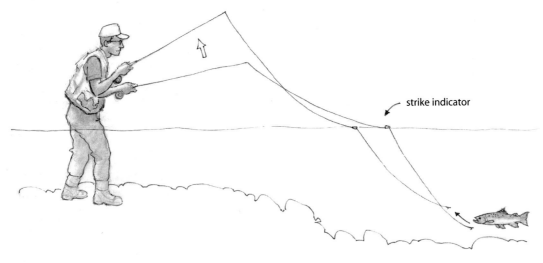

strike indicator

The Leisenring Lift is a specialized presentation of a nymph to a specific fish. You need to know exactly where the fish is holding, position yourself fairly close to the fish, and then lift the rod tip just as the drift brings the nymph in front of the fish, causing the nymph to rise. A rising nymph is a mature nymph and will trigger an immediate strike.

Where trout experience heavy fishing pressure, they're often conditioned by an overabundance of hooked artificials to ignore mature mayfly duns or adult caddisflies. This fact has given rise to the many emerger patterns now available and that can be very effective. Yet an older method of drifting a nymph just below the surface often outproduces these emerger patterns, and you're more likely to have the right nymph in your fly box than the right emerger.

Simply put, select a standard nymph pattern; that is, one without any extra weight or added brass or tungsten beads. Apply fly floatant—preferably the paste type rather than the spray-on or dip type—to 2 or 3 feet of your tippet just behind the fly to ensure that the nymph stays near the surface, but don't put any floatant on the fly itself because you want it to drift just below the meniscus. Then fish the nymph as you would a dry fly. This strategy is especially effective with caddisfly pupae.

You can determine when this is your best strategy by carefully watching the rise forms of the trout. If a trout is taking adults off the surface, you'll see a bubble in the middle of the rise ring, formed when the trout breaks the surface with his mouth. If the rise is for something just under the surface, the ring doesn't have this bubble and instead is formed from the bulge of water the fish pushes to the surface, or even by its back or tail as it turns back down. No bubble? Try a nymph near the surface.

Two other nymph strategies can be productive in specific, opposite stream conditions. The first is ideal when swimming nymphs are present in the quieter backwater bays or eddies of streams (or the still water of ponds or lakes) that they require. In

As we've emphasized before, rise rings are important because they tell us that trout not only are in a specific spot but are feeding, too. If we can see the ring well enough and there's a bubble in the middle of it, the trout has just taken his meal from the top of the surface. No bubble means that the trout has just eaten an emerger or nymph from just below the surface.

this circumstance, a sinking or sink-tip line is ideal, but in a pinch you can use a floating line. Once again you need to get the nymph to the bottom, but this time you want to mimic the movement of a swimming nymph, which means slowly retrieving the nymph along the bottom. Simply stripping in line will move the nymph too quickly. Remember, these are small organisms. So instead use the hand-twist method.

In the *hand-twist method* you gather a hand's width of line at a time by grabbing the line first with your thumb and forefinger and then twisting your hand to bring in line. Then grab the line with your little finger and twist again. This retrieve accomplishes two things. It gives the fly that swim-rest-swim action that perfectly imitates the natural, and it keeps you directly connected to the fly so that you'll feel any strike.

Finally, let's move from quiet water to hard, fast, deep flows of trout water. Often the biggest, strongest fish are holed up there, both because it's a safe place to be and because this is the kind of water that produces the biggest insects in the stream—stonefly nymphs.

The main advantage to the hand-twist method is that it slows down your retrieval. Because you're slowly twisting the line into your hand, your fly is moving in short and slow spurts, just as a natural does.

Obviously, the best nymph to fish in this circumstance is a big weighted stonefly. It will cast like a big rock, but it's what the fish will hit. The rising nymph method, and a variation of it, work well here. Use the rising nymph method when the hard flow is not much more than 3 feet deep, as is typical of the pocket water around big boulders. The fish will be holding behind the boulders or sometimes just in front of them, so the boulders are your targets. Cast far enough above a boulder so that the nymph sinks to the bottom. This is going to be quite a bit farther above your target area than you're used to because the fast-moving water will carry your nymph quickly downstream. Keep your rod pointed straight at your line and the nymph as they progress downstream and strip in line to keep the rod, line, and nymph aligned. (With this big nymph and these hard flows, an indicator is a useless hin-

Straight-line nymphing gives you a direct connection with your fly. In slow or moderate currents, you can cast up and across the stream and then mend your line to form a straight line. As the fly drifts back toward you, strip in excess line, all the while keeping your rod tip low. Any pause or twitch in the line may mean a take, but a short, quick strike will tell you if it is. If it isn't, you can lower the rod tip and continue the drift. As the fly gets past you, feed line back out.

drance.) At any pause in the fly, strike hard. Yes, it will be the bottom some of the time, but often enough it will be the largest fish in the stream.

When the hard-flowing water is deeper than 3 or 4 feet, you can use the variation of the rising nymph method. This time, however, you'll get only one rise of the nymph because the water is so fast and deep. Most of the time you'll need to cast upstream of your position, but with a fairly short line. As your line and the nymph pass in front of you, they should be at the correct depth, and because of the quickness of the flow you'll

In hard-flowing water, modify the straight-line method. Instead of stripping in line, raise the rod tip as the fly approaches a position directly opposite you to maintain a direct connection with it as it rolls along the bottom. As the fly gets past you, lower the rod tip to allow the line to feed back into the water. You still have that direct connection with the fly on the bottom.

need to raise your rod tip high to maintain contact with the fly. Don't pull the fly off the bottom—just maintain contact with it. And don't strip in line, because this will limit the length of the nymph's enticing drift. As it passes by, lower your rod tip again and then raise it once more at the end of the drift to give the nymph a swimming rise to the surface. Strikes can come anytime after the nymph is deep but will often occur at the end of the drift as the fly rises. And hold on: the combination of hard-flowing water and a big trout can be jolting.

STRATEGIES FOR WET FLIES AND STREAMERS

We've covered the rudimentary presentations of wet flies and streamers already, but as you may have guessed, there are additional strategies for improving their performance. The across-and-downstream method discussed earlier is still the best way to present both these types of underwater flies, and mending your line to get a uniform and perfect speed is necessary. As we've seen time and again, however, trout streams contain wide varieties of waters.

There are three basic varieties of wet flies: winged, wingless, and soft-hackled. Most of us immediately think of the traditional quill-winged wet flies that have been used for centuries. In duller and darker colors these can easily imitate adult caddis-flies, drowned mayfly duns, and dead or dying mayfly spinners. In addition, because of their wings they'll stay upright on the standard down-and-across swing and look just like adult caddisfly females returning to the surface.

Underwater insects aren't speed demons, however. Rarely will they take off for the middle of the stream or the far shore. More often they swim in little spurts, thrusting forward, then resting, then swimming again. We can imitate this action by manipulating our artificial, slowing its progress with an upstream mend and then either stripping in short lengths of line using the hand-twist method or raising and lowering the rod tip. Get your flies to swim erratically, and they'll look more real.

But when we want a winged wet fly to look more vulnerable—for example, when we suspect that fish are easily capturing meals from free-drifting food like dead or dying mayflies—it's more effective to dead-drift the fly like a nymph. Often a winged wet will draw a strike fished this way when nothing else will work. When a hatch of mayflies, especially in heavy flowing water, produces a number of drowned adult duns just below the surface film, they're easy meals for trout, they won't fly away, and winged wet flies imitate them nicely.

Wingless and soft-hackled wets are distinctly different from the winged varieties. Wingless wets have full bodies, usually of *dubbing* (fine fur) or peacock or turkey *herl*

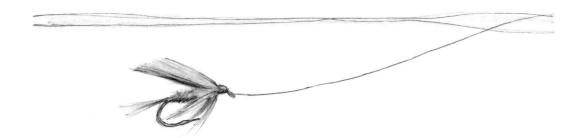

Winged wet flies are manipulated through the water to imitate mature egg-laying caddisflies and a few mayflies as they swim through the water column. The wing of the fly accomplishes two important things: It imitates the wing of the natural, and it tracks upright in the water, an important detail because the insects do the same thing.

(individual fibers from feathers). They look like full meals, and the turns of hackle at their throats imitate legs and provide enough motion to give them life. Soft-hackled wets are sparsely tied, with mere tying thread or floss for a body and long, soft hackle at their throats. Sometimes they have sparse bits of dubbing just behind the hackle. These flies depend on their soft hackle for motion and attraction (see photos next page).

These wet flies imitate nymphs and pupae caught in the current that are just struggling and drifting along or, more often, moving with a purpose—either getting themselves up in the water during behavioral drift or struggling to the surface to hatch. As with nymph imitations, raising our imitations up and down through the water column with the rod tip is a productive strategy. Their extra hackle, coupled with some action from the angler, makes them pulsate and look particularly enticing during their downstream drift.

Streamers, because they're bigger and imitate feed fish, need more motion than wet flies, but this motion is imparted in much the same way. On an across-and-downstream drift you can raise and lower the rod tip, or hand-twist the fly line, or strip in line more quickly. As a rule of thumb, the slower the current you're swimming a streamer through, the faster you need to retrieve it. But regardless of your retrieval method, let the streamer sit for a moment in the current downstream when the drift is finished, and then strip it upstream quickly. Often, this is when the strike will come, as it does in nature when a real forage fish panics and flees.

You might also dead-drift a streamer, especially below hard turbulence that might disorient a shiner or madtom, and especially in a dam tailwater where any number of feed fish are killed by turbines. New streamer patterns have been developed to float in imitation of these dead or disoriented fish, but even the old sinking patterns—when

Soft-hackled wet flies have two distinct advantages. First, their hackle closely imitates the legs of an insect, moving and fluttering in the water even when dead-drifted. Second, these flies imitate emerging or injured insects at or just below the surface. The sparse tie of these flies is often exactly like the insects they are intended to imitate. Here, a Partridge and Green *(left)* and a Leisenring Black Gnat *(right)*. *(Jim Dugan)*

free-drifted—will draw strikes. With the sinking patterns try a quick upward jerk of the rod and then let the fly dead-drift, thus imitating an injured feed fish.

Again, let your observations help you expand upon these ideas. If you're not drawing strikes from a particular method or a particular speed with wet flies or streamers, change the method or the speed. Do something different. But trust in these flies. They're ancient. They're effective. And, unfortunately, they're largely forgotten.

STILL-WATER STRATEGIES

In addition to the still-water fly fishing techniques discussed in chapter 5, there are a few specialized strategies for presenting artificial flies in still water. Because trout must keep moving to find food in still water, line control becomes critical. Although we often use the currents in a stream to make our flies look more lifelike, or must combat the effects of a current to do the same thing, still waters give us full and consistent control of the fly line and artificial. That means we must always be aware of how the fly is reacting to what we're doing with the fly line.

When fishing dry flies, our manipulation of the fly line often becomes a matter of studiously doing nothing. The fly must sit motionless on the surface because the trout have all the time in the world to examine it, and they'll often take an excruciatingly long time before deciding to strike. Long leaders—up to 15 feet long including tippet—are often necessary to get the fly out and away from the fly line.

Two pointers will help here. The first is to dress the fly thoroughly with floatant. On any one cast it may have to sit perfectly up on the water for several minutes. In addition, I put some paste floatant on about 3 feet of the tippet so it won't sink and cock the fly. Second, you need to keep the rod tip low and the line straight. A cruising trout can make a quick strike on a dry fly, and if you have too much slack in the line and your rod tip is high, it will be next to impossible to set the hook.

With underwater flies, it's what you do *after* you cast that gives the fly life. Still-water insects and forage move with varying degrees of speed. You need to make your flies do the same, and at the correct depth. Use the countdown method described in chapter 5 so that when you do find trout you can get to that same depth again and again. Then retrieve your fly according to the type of fly you've tied on. Swimming insects, such as Hexagenia mayfly nymphs and small crustaceans, swim in little spurts, so strip in no more than 6 inches of line at a time. Dragonfly nymphs squirt water from their abdomens that can propel them a foot or more rather quickly, so strip and pause to imitate that action. And feed fish, as in streams, dash and pause and can attract strikes when they seem panicked or injured, so vary your retrieval appropriately. Again, keep your rod tip low to the water so that you have full contact with the fly.

When fishing a dry fly in moving water, you often want slack in your line to prevent drag. On still waters, however, you want a straight line directly connecting you to your dry fly. Here, because the fish is moving and the water isn't, a rising trout can take a fly and expel it quickly if you don't have that direct connection. Any slack gives him that instant. A straight line will usually cause the fish to hook himself.

It may seem obvious, but you need to run your underwater flies through the water at the depth where the fish are holding. In spring, they'll be higher in the water column, so start there. In other words, retrieve your sinking line and flies a foot deep—say a three count—then 3 feet deep—say a ten count—and so on. In summer, however, start deep and work up. Find the bottom, or at least the tops of the weeds, by counting as the line sinks until it stops. Then on your next cast subtract some counts to get your nymph or streamer to glide along at the top of the weeds. Both methods will save time and put you onto fish much more quickly.

And yes, you can catch trout in larger bodies of water, but generally only in the spring or fall when they're in relatively shallow water. In the summer, when they hold in the depths, you probably can't reach them effectively. Fly fishing in water much deeper than 30 feet is difficult if not impossible unless you're trolling with all of your sinking fly line out plus some backing. And then there's that debate again about what constitutes fly fishing.

Don't shy away from still waters. They can seem daunting—there's so much water and so few obvious clues to where the fish are—but they can hold trout that are perfectly willing to take your flies, and the trout can be large and memorable.

Still waters can seem daunting to many fly fishers, but learning how to fish them in general and then applying your general knowledge to a specific body of water can produce exceptional catches. Big water is where big fish live.

9 | Trout Waters and Stream Safety

"But what is the test of a river? Who shall say? 'The power to drown a man,'
replies the river darkly."

R. D. BLACKMORE
TALES FROM THE TELLING-HOUSE, 1896

Now that you've been trout fishing for a while, you've seen that it's the water itself—its fertility, temperature, volume of flow, clarity, and its many other nuances—that most often affects trout and forage and how the trout respond to your offerings.

Too often we anglers don't appreciate or observe closely enough the effects of water composition or volume on trout and the aquatic organisms upon which trout depend. Sometimes, as on a spring creek or downstream from a dam that has just opened its gates (for both of these, read on), we're well aware of these effects. For the most part, however, we arrive at a stream with preconceived notions about how we're going to fish, and we don't spend enough time testing those notions against what the water is telling us.

Our earlier discussions of trout waters made little mention of their composition, of what constitutes fertile trout water and how that might change during the season or even during a day. It's time to look more closely at these things.

GROUNDWATER

Trout streams arise from two sources—runoff from snowmelt and rain and groundwater from springs. While we anglers can easily see the effects of a melting winter snowpack or a sudden downpour (see below), groundwater has the greater impact on the fertility and productivity of a trout stream.

Chapter 5 described three types of trout streams—spring creeks (also called limestone creeks or chalk streams), freestone streams, and tailwaters. Spring creeks and tailwaters represent ideal trout water, providing relatively stable water temperatures for trout year-round. Spring creeks also have that added slug of life-supporting minerals. But it's in freestone streams that we find ourselves standing most often, simply because there are so many more miles of them available.

These neat categories blur in practice, however, since nearly all freestone streams enjoy a beneficial admixture of groundwater seepage. While all groundwater seeps increase the health of a trout stream, they're not all created equal. Depending on the fraction of flow provided by these springs and the minerals contained in that water, the resulting enrichment of a freestone stream can be minimal or pronounced.

Even without minerals, springwater seeps in a freestone trout stream would be important because groundwater has seasonally stable temperatures that range, wherever trout are found, from 52 to 56°F. In winter months springs can provide enough warmer water to help trout survive, supplying havens from anchor ice or severely cold water. In summer they can provide the only places where trout *can* survive, because at water temperatures much above 75°F the dissolved oxygen in the water falls below levels that will keep trout alive. Quite simply, trout need cool water in order to

Freestone streams are the most variable of all trout waters. They can be big, as here, or small enough to jump over. They can meander and twist and turn, or they can plunge out of mountains in a torrent. But it is water quality—its purity and fertility—that offers their most telling details.

Stress for trout comes in the form of uncomfortable water temperatures, often accompanied by unusual water levels, high or low. To combat this stress, trout will seek out sources of water that are more comfortable. Here they've found a cool spring seep during the summer.

breathe. Usually trout are aggressively territorial, but when severe conditions prevail their focus is on survival, not territory, and they will abide close neighbors.

If you're treading the streambanks during these times of year—midwinter or midsummer—knowing where a major spring enters a stream means you know where to find trout. But if you choose to fish at these times, realize that any trout you catch may die from the encounter. Freezing cold winter air can irreparably harm the protective slime of a fish, while the already-stressed summer fish might simply suffocate or die from the shock of fighting in oxygen-depleted water. It's your choice.

For years, my choice has been to use these extreme times of year only to identify where major groundwater seeps exist. They're easy to identify in August, because that's where the trout will be gathered. Then, on the fringes of extreme weather, in spring and autumn, I can catch and release trout in these places without harming them.

When the groundwater entering a trout stream adds a healthy slug of minerals or nutrients, then an otherwise average freestone trout stream can become much more productive. Call it an enriched freestone stream. Without getting too technical, the minerals that enhance trout streams do so by buffering the effects of rainwater and runoff, which are naturally slightly acidic and have become much more so in the East due to air pollutants, some of which originate from industrial smokestacks in the Midwest. Just as you add limestone to your garden to sweeten the soil, groundwater that flows through calcium-containing rocks sweetens a trout stream. And this allows more plants and diatoms to grow, which in turn support more insects and trout forage. Remember how fertile spring creeks are? It's mainly because of the calcium-rich limestone.

Enriched freestone streams, then, support more life. And trout are at the top of the food chain, so there will be more of them in an enriched stream, in a broader variety of age classes. This will always be a help to you when choosing the streams in which you fish, your approach to them, and the flies you tie on. (See chapter 5.)

It becomes obvious that if we know where springwater flows into a trout stream, not only can we find plumes of water that the trout will use during seasonal extremes, summer or winter, but we can also identify sections of streams and tongues of water that will be at least somewhat more attractive as feeding and holding locations throughout the year. Discovering whether they exist at all in a favorite stream, and then pinpointing where the most important of them flow, adds another layer of interest in the way we approach and observe streams.

It also helps immeasurably to know about groundwater inflows when we find unusual water levels, either high or low. Although we know these conditions can prevail during spring runoff or the midsummer doldrums, they can and do occur at any time of year. Springs provide special havens then, too, and we can fish along their flows more successfully. (See below.)

Spring seeps that enter a trout stream directly in its bed, underwater, can be difficult to find. Small ones quickly mix in, and their effects are incremental. Larger ones, however, will induce a marked enrichment and higher trout populations downstream, often for quite some distance. That's why certain sections of streams may well be much more attractive to trout than others.

You can identify large springs by seeking out those rare spots in freestone streams that look like out-of-place underwater beaches. The upwelling water will raise sand

Where it flows into running or still water, groundwater offers several advantages, including consistent temperatures and enhanced mineral enrichment, both of which translate into more forage and more and bigger trout. Sandy underwater springs like this one, however, can be difficult to detect.

and silt with it, and there will be little opportunity for plants to take root. Expect more plants, more insects, and more trout downstream.

Those tiny feeder creeks that drip innocuously into a stream are important, too, because they usually originate as springs. In summer, any small runoff feeders will be dry, but where you find those sweet little flows of icy water, take a sip of them first, then think how well they enrich the water downstream.

At ideal water levels and temperatures in freestone streams, pinpointing spring seeps becomes much less important. In this case the trout stream is a veritable bank-to-bank flow of perfect water. In addition, where there are many small inflows of groundwater, as happens in many of the best trout streams, the mixing action of the current makes the water uniformly attractive, so pinpointing the springs becomes less crucial. In these enriched freestone streams supporting high numbers of trout and excellent forage, you can fish *all* of the water that might hold trout.

Groundwater is also important in still waters, and for many of the same reasons. You may remember the earlier discussion about finding cold-water sources in lakes and ponds. Groundwater provides comfort both for trout and for much of the forage on which trout depend, and it adds to the overall fertility of the water.

An awareness of the importance of groundwater will not only make us more effective anglers, but it will also help us to be better stewards of our water resources. Knowing that trout lakes and streams are complex accumulations of water supporting complex communities of plant and animal life, we see more clearly the importance of protecting these resources. (See chapter 10.) And primary among these resources are the aquifers that supply groundwater.

RISING WATER TO HIGH WATER

Rising water in a trout stream can be good or bad. A stream swelling with snowmelt will be so cold that the cold-blooded trout will be nearly inactive and hence unavailable to us. They'll find places in the stream where they're insulated to some degree from the cold, high water, places like spring seeps and deep holes, and there they'll wait out winter's last insult. This applies both to the early runoff, as the water rises, and throughout the time the water stays high.

I've fished the runoff, walking sloppy, snow-covered, treacherous banks. I've

Spring-fed feeder streams, like underwater groundwater seeps, enhance water fertility with their minerals. They also attract fish when the surrounding water temperatures get uncomfortable, often causing trout to prefer the plume of colder water where it enters a stream.

cast big, heavy nymphs into swollen streams and cleared ice from the eyelets of my fly rod. And I've studied the literature, reading the insistent avowals of experts that trout can be caught from runoff water. And I've come home from these experiences feeling good about getting out of the house to walk along familiar haunts, rod in hand and vest donned. I haven't caught many trout, however. Maybe even none. But don't be dissuaded. There are other reasons for trout fishing than catching trout.

It's important to note that where the snowpack piles high in the mountains, as it does in the Rockies, the pre-runoff spring angling is usually very good. Once the low natural flows in the valleys have warmed, there's good insect and trout activity. Spring

Fishing when runoff from the snowpack is rising or at its peak is rarely productive, except for the good it does getting you outdoors. As the water clears, however, even if it's still cold, the fish do begin to seek food actively. It can still be cold on the streambank, too, but the first fish of the year is often the most memorable.

angling in many of the famous trout waters of the West is marvelous because of this good action and because the tourist season, when the streams fill up with anglers, is still two or three months away. This is not so in the East, where runoff begins as soon as winter ends.

If you must fish during the winter or during the spring runoff—and I usually do because of an accumulation of what my brother-in-law Ron Lofland calls "fishing static"—go to a tailwater. I'm lucky to have a small tailwater near my home where the water comes from 70 feet below a dam. In winter it's 10 to 15°F warmer than naturally flowing stream water, and I've taken 3-pound browns on size 20 midges there in February.

In that same tailwater I'll turn right around and go home when the dam keeper releases water. The water below a dam release rises quickly—even dangerously on large rivers—and in my experience rising tailwaters shut down any fishing. This only makes sense. Trout that were working food drifts for nymphs or surface forage suddenly have a new problem. They must get out of the gush and behind a log or boulder or be washed downstream.

In addition, in tailwaters where the water level is severely manipulated, the forage is limited. If 2,500 cubic feet per second (cfs) of water is released when a dam is generating electricity, but the flow is cut back to 125 cfs when the gates are closed, there's not much water in the stream to support fish and forage. Only the streambed covered by the lowest flow, the 125 cfs, will produce aquatic insects. The rest of the streambed is dry land during low flows. Then, as the water rises during electrical generation, the fish disperse and the forage, what there is of it, is diluted. While this scenario is all too common, more and more dam owners are agreeing to supply minimum in-stream flows that approximate normal stream levels. They rely on surplus runoff water or

Tailwater fisheries can be good or bad. If minimum stream flows below a dam are severely low, forage is minimized and good trout habitat diminished. However, if run-of-river stream flows are the rule, where hydro operators generate electricity only with excess flows of water, then the stream below the dam benefits from uniform water levels that are often at ideal temperatures throughout the year.

rainstorm spates to turn their turbines, and the rivers below their dams are infinitely better served.

Slow, natural rises of water after spring runoff are another story, and a much better one. Those gentle spring and summer rainstorms that dimple a stream's surface are a joy. They don't usually reduce insect hatches. Indeed, if anything, they keep mayfly duns on the water longer because the mist and rain slow the drying of their wings. In some cases, as with Blue-Winged Olive mayfly hatches, the flies prefer that overcast, damp weather and will wait for it before emerging. As important, we anglers are much less obvious to trout when the surface of the water is ruffled with rain—not that clear window of laminar water out of which trout so easily see.

In addition, gentle rainfalls are signals to trout that food is about to become more abundant. Not only will the trout have their normal and natural aquatic insect meals on which to feed, but uncounted terrestrial organisms will get washed into the stream, too, especially early in a rainstorm and as the small feeder streams also rise.

When trout stream waters are slowly rising, you rarely need to do anything differently from fishing in normal water flows other than enjoy the trout that are rising

Low-water flows below dams can be much more harmful than natural low-water flows, because they occur irregularly and unnaturally. A river flowing at full spate that is suddenly cut to a fraction of its normal flow leaves little time, and few locations, for river life—forage and trout—to adjust.

leisurely to hatching mayflies. I've found that these trout are not as selective as usual. Maybe they've discovered that anglers are as sparse during rain as hatches are easy to feed on. Either match the hatch or fish with nymphs as you normally would during pre- and posthatch periods, and always carry some Blue-Winged Olive Dun imitations and Pheasant Tail Nymphs. These insects love damp misty weather and emerge, East or West, throughout the year.

If no hatch is present or impending, use terrestrials—ants, inchworms, beetles, crickets, or grasshoppers. Make them small early in the season, as these insects often haven't matured. Later you can use larger, winged ants and full-sized beetles and hoppers.

If the rise of water is gentle and increases the stream flow only minimally at its peak, just relish the opportunity. If the rain is more substantial and the resulting rise more pronounced, fish hard as the water is coming up. The fish are aware of the impending change, probably because of the increased sediment and debris in the water but also because of the increased food items that are washing by. They'll feed heavily and on a wide variety of food, so offer big mouthfuls that will attract their attention. Good choices are Woolly Worms or Buggers, or big Hare's Ear or stonefly nymphs (see chapter 12).

As the water discolors during fast rises and heavy flows, the trout will seek refuge from the energy-sapping heavy rush. Now is the time to use those high-water techniques of slow, thorough angling. The trout will be near cover, close to the streambank, behind boulders or logs, and within the safe haven of spring seeps. They'll still actively feed if they can, but their striking range will be reduced as their vision is reduced and their need to stay out of heavy flows increases. Put your deep-running nymphs, wet flies, or streamers down on the bottom of the stream and fish those areas where the trout can take advantage of them. Just remember that the trout in this heavy water are especially aware of the energy equation and will only take advantage of the smorgasbord that's drifting by if they don't have to spend too much energy to get to the food.

FALLING WATER TO LOW WATER

Once the water has peaked and starts to drop, several good things happen. First and foremost, the water clears and—depending on how long it was high, how roiled it was, and how available drifting food items were—the trout will be anxious to resume their normal positions and feeding habits. Often they'll be hungry. The forage, too, will get back to business as usual because in high water the survival instinct takes hold and few hatches occur. As the water clears and drops, hatches can be heavy while an accumulation of mayflies and caddisflies that have held off emerging start to catch up. The trout will return to the holding and feeding lanes that offer them their best advantage, and they'll quickly resume feasting.

When fishing a stream at low water levels, relearn it as if you'd never seen it before. Runs and pools that were productive at normal levels will be abandoned as the water drops and exposes the fish to more danger. Likewise, deep resting pools at normal water levels may now take on more importance as feeding and foraging sites. At the very least, trout and forage may be more concentrated in low water, and the angling can be exceptional.

Much more subtle changes occur as trout streams fall below their normal water levels. While we've discussed earlier how stressful low water can be in midsummer when the water is warm, low flows may occur at any time of year. Below-normal snowpacks can lower streams early; spring droughts, although rare, are not unheard of; but most often low-water conditions of summer stretch into the autumn.

When high water temperatures are not a factor, low water levels can create some excellent angling if you know where to look. Both the fish and the forage move and become concentrated. Areas that were productive holding waters at full flow become barren of fish when the water is too shallow for protection. Because trout need both food and safety, they'll seek new areas. Productive pieces of water that you so carefully scouted at full flow are often abandoned when the water is low.

Deeper water is necessary, so concentrate on what might have been fast-flowing, unproductive runs before but have now become attractive, or on the deepest pools or the most deeply undercut banks. The feeding lanes will change as the water drops and will be more widely disbursed, but there often will be higher concentrations of trout and forage. Use the same stream-craft skills you deploy when approaching new water. Quite simply, you need to relearn where the best water and the trout are located, but low-water flows make this process easier, and the rewards can be great.

STREAM SAFETY—AGAIN

Chapter 2 offered counsel on how to survive a dunking. To recap, have your wading belt cinched tight; get your face up and your feet pointing downstream; wait for a place where you can get your feet back under you; and don't panic.

When you fish in summer, in cold water, and during rising water, however, there are a few more hazards that you need to be aware of. While I'd like to say, "just use common sense," some of these hazards are sudden, while others are subtle. Remaining alert to them will help you fish safely and happily.

The most sudden of these hazards is lightning. I was on a stream in Maine two miles from my vehicle when a thunderstorm just plain built on top of me. That first roll of thunder and simultaneous lightning bolt got my attention in a hurry. Hustling back toward the truck, I felt the hair on the back of my neck literally stand up just three seconds before a crashing bolt split a tree not a hundred feet from me. I had just enough time to throw my rod off to the side.

Yes, I threw the rod. Fly rods are made of graphite and conduct electricity, and they can attract lightning quite effectively, especially if you're standing in open water. They are also 8 or 9 feet long or longer. Get out of the water, and if you can't make it quickly back to your vehicle or a building, lay the rod on the ground and get a hundred yards

When rumbles of thunder begin or a storm approaches, take note and seek cover. Remember that lightning can strike several miles from the storm itself, and bear in mind that graphite rods are excellent conductors of electricity, like 9-foot-long lightning rods. Don't delay, even if that's the biggest trout you've seen all day.

away from it. Go to low ground, away from the tallest trees, and wait out the storm.

Cold weather or wading too long in cold water can bring on hypothermia by gradual degrees; a cold-water dunking can bring it on in a rush. Hypothermia is a lowering of the body temperature to dangerous levels. First the shivers hit, then a general peaceful feeling ensues as your body shuts down its extremities. Walking will be difficult. Speech will be slurred. Unconsciousness will follow. And if the core temperature of your torso and organs falls too far, you will die.

The best way to fight hypothermia is to prevent it. Wear layers of clothing and pay attention to your body. Shivering is a way for the body to generate heat. It means that you're getting cold. Get to a heat source if you can, or build a fire, or drink some hot coffee, hot chocolate, or soup. Just don't ignore your shivering.

If you've gotten wet, you need to get out of the wet clothes. The chilling effect of soaked clothes continues as long as they make contact with your skin. Have a spare set of clothing with you or nearby in your vehicle, and change into it as soon as you can.

As mentioned earlier, fishhooks can and will impale you. You can combat this by wearing safety glasses, shirts and jackets with collars, and a hat, but it's still possible to get a hook in your hand, neck, or arm. It's always best to have a doctor remove a hook, especially from a vulnerable area such as your face or neck, and the operation will be much less painful with a nice shot of novocaine dulling the flesh around the wound.

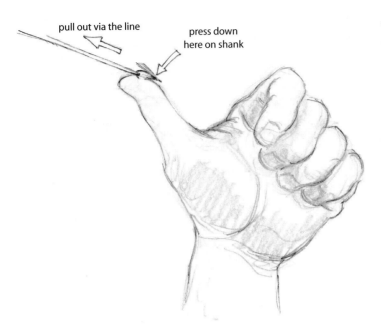

pull out via the line

press down
here on shank

Removing a barbed hook from the fleshy part of an arm, hand, or back is not difficult. Loop a piece of twine or line under the hook shank and snug it to the bend. Press down on the shank of the hook to get the barb to follow the path it has already made—and not cut its way back out—and then give a quick yank. Don't try to remove a hook that is near an artery (the neck) or the eyes.

But if you're off in the wilderness, other measures are needed. I once had to remove an artificial grasshopper from the thumb of a lady who was being kind enough to show me some of her best cutthroat water. Here's how you do it. Loop a piece of stout line (I used fly line) under the shank of the hook and against its bend. Push down on the shank of the hook and yank the point of the hook and the barb up and out as shown. You're attempting to get the hook to follow the entry wound in reverse, and holding the shank down will keep the barb from doing more damage. If all goes well, it will pop right out with only a single drop of blood, as it did for the lady I assisted.

Although I mostly fished alone when I was young and foolish, now I'm much more comfortable when a friend comes along. Companions can prevent little mishaps from turning into disasters. And wherever and whenever I'm fishing, alone or with a partner, someone always knows where I am and when to expect me back.

Be careful when you're fly fishing, and you'll make marvelous memories of the glorious outdoors.

10 | The Future of Fly Fishing

"No sport affords a greater field for observation and study than fly fishing, and it is the close attention paid to the minor happenings upon the stream that marks the finished angler."

GEORGE M. L. LA BRANCHE
THE DRY FLY AND FAST WATER, 1914

Now that you've become a fly fisher, your focus has evolved from a small circle of interest, roughly defined by the length of your cast, to a much broader appreciation of the expansive yet fragile world that beckons you beyond that circle. You've learned that trout and trout waters are rare, complex, and mysterious; that wild trout and fertile trout streams are rarer still; and that without personal, local, regional, and national policies based on the highest possible ethical standards toward trout waters, these fisheries are easily diminished and too often destroyed.

These high standards must begin with the individual. Because each of us stands in the middle of his or her own circle, the ripples we create—like the rings of a rising trout—expand outward and touch all whom we encounter while fishing. If we show respect for other anglers, we can expect the same courtesy in return.

Likewise, we can each have an impact on access to lakes and streams. The respect we show in our access to good water—in walking along its banks and crossing public and private land—reflects our appreciation of the privilege. Leaving the land as good as or better than we found it may create only small ripples of appreciation, but you may be sure that littering or abusing the land will create tidal waves of opposition to letting future anglers near the water.

Beyond our personal conduct, trout waters face larger challenges, and combating them requires cooperation both among anglers and with other groups that hold the health and vibrancy of flowing and still waters as their primary concern.

All over the country, small conservation groups have won major victories restoring and preserving local waters. A small group with a focused goal and a strong voice can (figuratively speaking) move mountains.

Regional groups are powerful when they create groundswells throughout an area or watershed for remediation and protection. A group that recognizes that many of our most important waters easily cross artificial political boundaries can bring about lasting change for the benefit of all.

And national groups give a unified and strong voice to both local and regional issues, in addition to focusing attention on continental and even international issues.

We look at local, regional, and national conservation groups later in this chapter. The active participation of each individual fly fisher is essential for preserving what we have, remediating past wrongs, and expanding our opportunities to fish.

Good trout waters are finite assets that demand our best stewardship. Each angler can help ensure access to these waters by showing the highest respect for the asset itself and for those landowners whose property abuts good trout water. Leave an area better off than you found it and the landowner genuinely pleased to see that you respect and value his courtesy. If you don't, signs like these will sprout overnight.

STREAM ETIQUETTE

Fly fishing is an intensely personal experience. Each of us has his or her own reasons for drifting off onto a trout pond or walking a streambank, for watching a rise of mayflies or a rise of mist. Some want to catch as many trout as possible. Others want to hook and handle the largest trout a water has to offer. But most of us feel lucky just to be at our leisure outdoors.

Usually, our motives are mingled: to be alone; to compare experiences with others; to see a deer, a loon, or a rare wildflower; to read a current; to identify a hatch or stage of a hatch; to pick the right fly; to make a decent cast; to feel the flow of water on our legs; to hold, for a moment, a wild fish; to appreciate a beautiful piece of water; to lose the passage of time in the rhythms of a stream. . . . To fish.

These impulses and others occupy our hours on the stream, sometimes subconsciously and sometimes in revolving primacy as an afternoon wears on. Yet rarely do they coincide with those of other anglers encountered astream. If I'm concentrating on a precise presentation to a fish or studying the smutting rise of a brown trout, I will certainly not appreciate someone, friend or stranger, wading into the pool beside me for a friendly chat or an exchange of theories. In fact, I'll consider it downright rude and a breach of stream etiquette. I would never interfere with someone's enjoyment of the sport, whether or not his objectives coincided with mine, unless invited.

The reading of that invitation may be the most difficult skill of all to acquire on trout water. Trout, for all our fascination with them, are fairly straightforward creatures—they eat, survive, reproduce. But the human animal is a complex and emotional being. Does that angler want to chat or not? Do I? A simple, short greeting or response often reflects a preference for solitude, and that wish must always be respected.

Respect for fellow anglers should govern our actions in other ways, too. For instance, a simple rule in trout streams is that an angler fishing upstream has the right of way. I like fishing wet flies downstream, but if I encounter an angler casting his flies upstream and heading my way, he has the right of way, and I'll reel in and let him pass. Likewise, if I get to a favorite pool or stretch of stream only to find it already occupied by an angler working the water or even sitting streamside and just watching, it's his water. Only if he initiates conversation or offers the pool to me will I consider fishing it. If I were to ask outright if I could fish the pool, I'd be inappropriately elbowing my way in. If I ignore this protocol, his fishing experience will be diminished and mine will never meet my expectations.

The list goes on. Don't gloat when you're catching fish. It's tacky. You'll experience days when others are catching fish and you aren't, and then you'll understand.

Good anglers often share information and flies. Do the same if the opportunity presents itself.

Realize that the best interactions with other anglers often come when you're gearing up or breaking down. Be receptive to their ideas and share your own, but don't mistake a parking lot exchange for an invitation to ignore stream etiquette.

Never, ever, leave any trash, yours or others'. If you carried a candy bar and a soda in, carry an empty wrapper and can out. Realize that any fishing line, but especially monofilament leader material, can be deadly. It's easy to wrap up excess line and stuff it in a pocket, and I consider it essential to retrieve line attached to flies lost in trees or bushes. Too many times I've found birds entangled.

Always extend your respect for trout waters to the land they abut. While opportunities to reach good trout water are expanding, the vast majority of the land is still privately owned, and we walk across it only through the generosity of a landowner. Insult him by disrespecting his generosity, and that access will shut down in a heartbeat. And there are already too many of us crowding too few places to fish.

Never cross through croplands or hayfields. Always use the edges. Leave gates and fences as you found them. Approach landowners and ask permission to cross their land to fish. Leave your name and address as a courtesy. And leave their land, and their attitude toward anglers, in better shape than you found it.

This code of conduct does not reflect some stuffy elitist attitude. Rather, it reveals our appreciation of the rare gift

The most valuable insurance for access to good trout water is often bought with sweat equity. Here, anglers have erected a simple ladder that makes the landowner appreciative and other anglers happy that they don't have to navigate barbed wire.

that trout waters represent and the value that we place on those too few times when we can enjoy that gift.

Equally important, as fly fishers' respect for the resource expands, so too does the influence each of us can exert for the benefit of all waters. By combining our voices with those of other anglers and stewards of clean, pure waters, we can create an ever more powerful call for preserving and restoring our waters.

LOCAL CONSERVATION

It's difficult to overstate the effectiveness of a group of voices focused on one issue. When one angler grumbles about this useless dam or that pipe of parking lot runoff, he might be seen as a quirky hermit. But when two voices carry the message, and the message is well thought out and appropriate, they make a force to be reckoned with. Swell those two voices to a local group, and good things can happen fast.

I thought long and hard about the order of this chapter, progressing as it does from the individual to large national and international groups, and I'm certain I'm presenting it in descending order of importance. Individual ethics and stewardship are of primary importance because they form the bedrock of any movement to put our trout resources first. Small local groups and coalitions are next in importance because they can accomplish so much in a local region. The smallest feeder streams must be healthy, or the entire river system suffers.

Although I've fished all over the United States and Canada, I can't hope to list the areas that should and do concern local anglers across the continent. Only local anglers can know which issues are most pressing. Here in New England, however, many fights to remove old and useless dams on premium waters have been fought successfully. There are many more to fight. And although some of the most famous dam removals, like the Edwards Dam on Maine's Kennebec River, did welcome and benefit from the help of larger national organizations, they started with small local groups identifying a wrong and pressing for its remediation.

Closer to my home, a long fight by a coalition of small local groups, who convinced local politicians of its importance, brought about a Massachusetts rivers protection piece of legislation that keeps new development at least 250 feet away from flowing water.

In my hometown, many of us have lobbied for a strong town conservation commission that has real power to veto any project that might jeopardize the little brook-trout stream that flows along the entire length of the community. In addition, we're still fighting to remedy the damage done to a tailwater fishery when the dam that created it

More and more waters have guaranteed access through fee title or easement purchases by fish and game departments or private clubs or organizations. With this guaranteed access often comes guaranteed angling pressure. By imposing strict limits or catch-and-release regulations, managers are trying to balance angling pressure with the available resource. Ignoring these regulations can only diminish the experience for everyone.

was built. During the dam's construction back in the 1930s, the Swift River was dredged into a featureless canal for a mile downstream from the Quabbin Reservoir, which supplies drinking water to Boston. We're trying to restore it to riparian health.

For local groups to be effective, they need to recognize the sources of problems and lobby for their resolution. In the East, these sources include thermal pollution from highways, parking lots, dense housing, and useless dams; groundwater pollution from substandard septic tanks or archaic sewer systems; improperly sited or regulated developments such as ski resorts on critical watersheds; feeder streams denuded of trees by timber harvesters; withholding of appropriate minimum water flows below power generating dams; and so on, into what sometimes seems a never-ending list.

Elsewhere in the country, you can add destruction of riparian habitat by overgrazing livestock along and in streams; water withdrawals for irrigation wherever agriculture is present in the East, Midwest, and West; roads built too close to streams or even through them; crudely bulldozed logging roads that choke upland streams on public and private land with mud and silt; and hatchery-reared trout displacing wild trout.

Wherever you live, there's no lack of local issues to draw your attention, and personal involvement in protecting good trout water or returning it to health is no less an achievement than catching your first trout on a fly.

To which groups should you donate time and dollars? All of them, if you could, but most of us can't. So be discerning. Being inactive in ten groups is not as valuable as being a strong and active advocate in one. I like my local Trout Unlimited chapter (Pioneer Valley) because its members are proactive environmentalists and superb trout fishers. There's also a local watershed association that has actively sought and acquired a federal Wild and Scenic River designation for a Western Massachusetts river system, protecting it from further development. And even the local fish and game club has purchased a broad swath of river frontage and keeps it clean and open to the public. Look locally, identify a need that's not being met or needs to be addressed, and either join a group or start one. But get active.

REGIONAL CONSERVATION GROUPS

Regional and statewide conservation groups have at least two important functions. First, they offer the strong voice of coalitions of smaller local groups. And second, they serve as important watchdogs over the local and state public agencies with direct authority over our natural resources.

When like-minded outdoorspeople make common cause with groups voicing more general concerns for our limited natural resources, the combined voice of these local groups in a regional coalition, especially when focused on a particular issue, is often impossible to ignore. Whether formed as temporary coalitions to address single important issues or as permanent partnerships to accomplish ongoing tasks, regional groups are important.

Focusing on the specific issues of anglers is important to preserving, protecting, and enhancing water resources, and often regional or statewide coalitions of anglers are surprisingly strong. Add hunters and trappers to a coalition, and the group can wield significant influence. The Sportsman's Alliance of Maine (SAM), for example, is an influential advocate for its members' interests in the proceedings of Maine's Department of Inland Fisheries and Wildlife (DIF&W), and it also lobbies the state legislature as well as the DIF&W with proactive ideas about Maine's vast outdoors.

When the voices of all river and watershed users form a group, even if the group is only a temporary, one-issue coalition, real change is possible. For instance, when all the dams on one Vermont and Massachusetts blue-ribbon trout stream, the Deerfield River, came up for relicensing, a coalition of public agencies and private user groups hammered out an agreement with the dam owners that created conservation easements on thousands of acres of watershed lands to protect upland feeder streams and remote hiking trails, increased minimum water flows below the dams to protect trout and forage, and established lower water flows early and late in the day for anglers and higher water flows at midday for rafters and kayakers, among other things. The agreement was in place when relicensing hearings began before the Federal Energy Regulatory Commission (FERC), only the second time in history that this had happened in the United States. The hearings were speedy and avoided the often contentious confrontations and unpredictable results of a regulatory process.

The list of examples could certainly go on, but the message is clear. Although we fly fishers are often seen as narrow-minded, single-topic advocates of better trout water and angling, when you combine a large number of voices with other groups having the vibrant health of lakes, rivers, and streams at heart, the resultant political and social clout is formidable.

OK, one more example. The Sportsman's Alliance of Maine and the Natural Resources Council of Maine (NRCM) worked together with other local, state, and national groups for the above-mentioned removal of the Edwards Dam from the Kennebec River, even though these two groups sometimes differ on other issues.

And that raises another point. SAM, NRCM, and other regional and statewide groups have staff who know the laws, the precedents, the regulatory processes, and the political forces involved, and who are paid to lobby legislators, testify at public hearings, draft position papers, sit through depositions, participate in stakeholder groups, and hurdle or bypass the other obstacles conservation groups encounter. When you're a volunteer advocate for a local group, taking time from your day job to attend meetings and hearings, you'll learn to appreciate the significance of this. At some point you'll look around a crowded room and realize that you're the only participant who's not being paid to be there, and you'll suddenly realize how steep the road ahead really is. That's why, for example, NRCM's help was critical to the tiny, all-volunteer Georges River Tidewater Association's successful efforts to force improvements on two municipal wastewater treatment plants on the St. George River in Maine. What GRTA brought to their partnership was local visibility, a sharp focus on a local issue, and the credibility that state regulators are inclined to grant to citizens who have not lobbied them on other issues in the past. That's why, in a coalition of local and regional groups, the whole is greater than the sum of its parts.

NATIONAL GROUPS

The line between local, regional, and national groups interested in protecting and restoring trout waters and watersheds is often indistinct. Good national groups are well aware of the critical needs, resources, and closely focused eyes of regional and local groups, particularly anglers and river and lake stewards, and they provide aid in many ways.

Their premier advantage is the political, social, and economic clout they can bring to the table when it comes to defending and restoring natural resources. And when national groups, both private and public, form coalitions to address issues of importance to all outdoors lovers, they can produce a strong voice of advocacy and a power of real substance.

I can recommend a few diverse national groups with proven track records in natural resource preservation and remediation. (See the resources section for contact information.) Please don't think this list is exhaustive. It's limited by my experience with trout and trout waters. Many other superb conservation groups are doing excellent work on behalf of freshwater fish like walleye, pike, and bass; saltwater fish like stripers, bluefish, billfish, and groundfish; and rivers, lakes, estuaries, and watersheds. Other groups have an overarching interest in wild lands as their focus. Certainly you have to be discerning, but above all you should be as active as possible with your time and money.

At the top of my personal list is Trout Unlimited. Its national offices are just outside Washington, D.C., but TU's effectiveness comes from its 125,000 members and 500 local chapters. Their mission statement is quite simple and to the point: "to conserve, protect and restore North America's trout and salmon fisheries and their watersheds."

The list of TU projects and accomplishments, and more specifically those of its local chapters, is impressive: dam removal, stream revival, in-stream flow assurances and advocacy, riparian habitat protection and restoration, sea-run salmon advocacy on both coasts, outreach programs in the form of a fine magazine and TV show, and more. I especially appreciate their from-the-ground-up approach. Not only do they listen to their members, but they know that their local chapters and individual members form their strength. They encourage local and regional action, and each member has a voice. And they're doing good and important work.

Trout waters, however, are best when they arise out of natural watersheds, from small, cold, mountain and hillside feeders merging into brooks, then streams, then rivers. And more and more, devotees are realizing that to preserve and enhance trout waters, you need to preserve and enhance entire watersheds.

This fact broadens the scope of our range of interest and support to include conservation groups—both public and private—that embrace this broader view. From the U.S. Fish and Wildlife Service to the semipublic Conservation Fund to private organizations like the Nature Conservancy and the Trust for Public Land, many groups with broad views about conserving entire ecosystems, bit by bit or in their entirety, require our attention and deserve our support.

Our attention needs to be focused especially on the public trustees of our public lands. We need to ensure that our local parks departments are always moving toward enhancement of our resources; that state environmental agencies, which more and more hold sway over forest and public wildlands, always know that they are advocates, not developers; and that the federal bureaucracies that exercise dramatic nationwide influence over huge swaths of our natural resources—agencies like the Forest Service and the Bureau of Land Management—have an influential block of voters and advocates examining their moves and motives.

Private national conservation groups do have economic clout, yet they can never approach the assets of our public agencies. What these private groups can do successfully is facilitate important preservation efforts, often jumping in and acting quickly while government agencies lumber toward action or try to evade it.

For example, a large chunk of northern New Hampshire came up for sale recently. International Paper (IP) decided to sell 171,500 acres that covered almost all of Pittsburg, New Hampshire, the largest township in area east of the Mississippi River, plus parts of two other towns, Clarksville and Stewartstown. The acreage covered nearly the entire watershed of the Connecticut Lakes Region, long famous as a fishing destination and the birthplace of New England's longest river, the Connecticut. The land includes 840 miles—yes, miles—of brooks and streams.

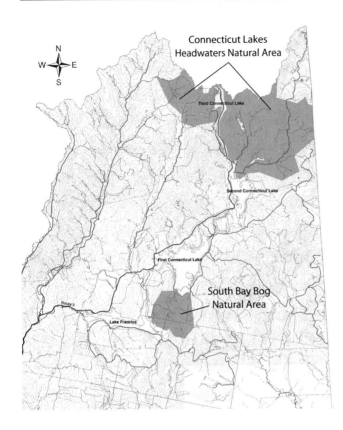

Connecticut Lakes
Headwaters Natural Area

Third Connecticut Lake

Second Connecticut Lake

First Connecticut Lake

Route 3

Lake Francis

South Bay Bog
Natural Area

The cooperative effort of many groups and the state government of New Hampshire brought about the quick protection of one of fishing's most dazzling areas: 171,500 acres of prime watershed and recreational lands in the Connecticut Lakes District. This area is now under conservation easement yet remains a working forest. While specific details of the deal took longer, money was raised and deeds transferred in less than six months. *(The Trust for Public Land)*

More and more in recent times, converting capital assets into cash, and quickly, is considered essential to the survival of many big companies, especially those in the volatile forest products and paper industries. IP couldn't (or wouldn't) wait for the slow machinations of public agencies.

A local coalition quickly formed. The Society for the Protection of New Hampshire Forests, which was established in 1901, helped create the Connecticut Lakes Headwaters Partnership Task Force, and both realized that this was a rare opportunity to preserve the crown jewel of New Hampshire's watersheds. They acted decisively. They brought in the Trust for Public Land, which met IP's asking price and bought the land with cash and loans. A conservation easement was immediately placed to restrict any further subdivisions or development on the land and to ensure public access. The Nature Conservancy added important financial clout when it purchased 25,000 acres of critical wildlife and watershed habitat destined to be transferred to the state's Fish and Game Department. And with the easements in place and the most critical lands protected, a New Hampshire timber company of long established stability, the Lyme Timber Company, offered to buy the remaining land to keep it a working forest, ensuring the tax base upon which the local communities depended and keeping the townspeople working in the woods.

The quick action of the private groups worked. The land was put up for sale on July 1, 2001, and by January 2002, only six months later, the transfer was completed and the land preserved. As if to put an exclamation point on how slowly such a complex deal can evolve, the 25,000-acre transfer to the Fish and Game Department occurred on July 1, 2003, and the details and financing necessary to transfer the rest of the forest to the Lyme Timber Company were completed in October 2003.

None of this preservation would have been possible without the decisive action of private local and national groups or without the speedy formation of a coalition that could bring vision to the project as well as economic and political clout.

Pittsburg, New Hampshire, offers a prime example of how good preservation efforts can benefit all anglers. It also helps that in these Connecticut River headwaters, wild and holdover trout are available in miles and miles of streams and thousands of acres of lakes and ponds. Plus you can almost always spot a moose meandering along.

I fished in the Connecticut River this spring above Lake Francis. The water levels were perfect, the trout were abundant and big, and the moose along Route 3 above Pittsburg were plentiful and awe-inspiring. Knowing that this area hadn't changed much in a hundred years made the trip memorable, but knowing that it was now preserved for at least that much longer gave me a renewed respect and appreciation for the many individuals who had brought real conservation to the region—anglers and nature lovers all.

The degree to which each of us is willing or able to become involved in ensuring an ample supply of trout water in the near and far future is a personal decision. You can start by developing a personal respect for our resources and displaying that respect through your actions on any trout stream. When you become a devoted fly fisher, you should become involved at some higher level, too, whether you purchase a membership in your local TU chapter, participate in stream cleanup or enhancement projects, or even become a local, regional, or national leader and voice advocating for vibrant streams, healthy lakes, and protected watersheds.

PART THREE

GOING FARTHER
AND
FURTHER

11 | Beyond Trout

"When Salar *soars, diamond-bedecked,
I do not bow, I genuflect."*

JACK FALLON
"CHERISH THE LEAPERS," IN GRAY'S SPORTING JOURNAL,
FEBRUARY/MARCH 2003

Trout are at the heart of fly fishing. The sport originated in pursuit of trout hundreds of years ago, and trout will always preoccupy fly fishers, largely because of where the fish live, what they eat, and how they react to their natural forage and our attempts to imitate it. By extension, fly fishers find similar fascination with migrating anadromous salmonids—Atlantic and Pacific salmon and steelhead trout. Especially with Atlantic salmon, a long tradition of fly fishing exists, and practitioners have never doubted that salmon are the kings of gamefish.

In the last thirty years, however, the world of fly fishing has expanded like a tidal wave. Largely because of advances in affordable fly rod and reel technology, nearly any fish that swims in fresh or salt water can now be caught with feathers and fur.

Because the tackle is easily available and because innovative fly tiers have developed plausible imitations of preferred forage, fly fishing in fresh water for black bass, northern pike and pickerel, catfish and carp, and panfish has become widespread and popular.

In addition, fly rods that can handle heavy fly lines up to weight 14 and cast very large flies are now widely available. Not only can they cast the big flies, but these stalwart rods have the backbone to fight ocean-sized fish. Likewise, fly reels are now large enough to hold ample line and backing and have sophisticated and strong drag systems to match the strength of the rods and the fish. You can now target billfish and sharks with a fly rod in blue waters, but you'll more likely find a striped bass or bluefish at the end of your line. And they're no pushovers.

Yes, trout are still at the heart of fly fishing, but you'll do yourself a great disservice if you don't expand your interests to include any of these other exciting gamefish.

SALMON AND STEELHEAD

Salmon and steelhead are anadromous salmonids that live and feed in the ocean and spawn in freshwater streams. Because they spend much of their lives in the ocean, they can grow large, and because they migrate up into freshwater rivers and streams, they are readily available to anglers. Their attraction to fly fishers is their willingness to take a fly, and when hooked, they put up strong and often spectacular fights.

On the eastern North American coast, only Atlantic salmon are available, and in recent years their range and numbers have been dropping dramatically. Dams, water and genetic pollution, commercial overharvesting, and changing North Atlantic conditions have all contributed to this decline. Once Atlantic salmon could be found spawning in freshwater flows from Long Island to Labrador, but now they are largely extirpated from the United States, and their runs are much diminished in many parts of Canada.

This plight has not gone unnoticed by Canada and the United States, and strong efforts involving extensive research and large sums of money have been undertaken to halt the decline and restore populations. Progress has been painfully slow, however, with only minor victories, and the ultimate survival of the species remains in the balance.

While there is virtually no angling for sea-run Atlantic salmon in the United States, there are still a number of watersheds in Canada where the fish are holding their own. In New Brunswick, Quebec, Newfoundland, and Labrador good runs of salmon still attract anglers from across the continent. Fly fishing is the law in most, if not all, of the Atlantic salmon's range.

The attraction of fishing for Atlantic salmon revolves around two facts. First, the

Atlantic salmon have a long and storied history of being pursued with the fly rod. Here, a 12-pound ready-to-breed male salmon (the hook on his jaw, called *kype*, reveals him to be a breeding male) is readied for release.

fish do not eat after they have entered fresh water, except when they are returning to the sea after overwintering under river ice. (Unlike Pacific salmon, Atlantic salmon can survive spawning and return another year to spawn again.) Pushing up into fresh water from spring to autumn, the salmon at first would seem unlikely subjects for fly fishing. And yet, for unknown reasons, they do strike at flies, flies that over the centuries have gained as much mystery as the fish. The flies rarely imitate any particular food item. In fact, favored patterns differ from river to river and even pool to pool.

Second, the fight of a hooked Atlantic salmon is a marvel to behold. Strong, sleek fish with oversized tails, Atlantic salmon make hard, fast, long runs and spend much of their fighting time in the air. In fact, their scientific name, *Salmo salar*, translates into "salmon leaper." Only if you have been on one end of a fly rod with a mature Atlantic on the other can you fully appreciate their strength, stamina, and raw energy.

Atlantics are usually fished by casting a wet salmon fly down and across the current on a long line. The fly sweeps across holding water, showing its profile, and perhaps on the first cast (but usually on the hundredth), a salmon for some reason sweeps up from the depths in a boil of water to look at and perhaps take the fly. Salmon are also fished with dry flies, often clipped deer hair concoctions that again rarely imitate anything specific, and a rising fish seems incongruous as its huge jaws close on a tiny fly.

Atlantic salmon fishing has a long and storied history and a tradition both in North America and in Europe unlike any other. The literature and lore continually celebrate

Atlantic salmon flies like these are unique, their invention and design limited only by the fly tier's imagination. When mature salmon enter fresh water on their spawning run, their esophagi close and they don't feed. Why they strike at a fly remains a mystery.

When hooked, an Atlantic salmon requires all the skill an angler can muster. Long, strong runs are punctuated with spectacular leaps. *Bowing to the fish*—that is, lowering the rod tip when the fish is airborne—is essential to prevent the fish from snapping the tippet when it thrashes in the air or lands back in the water, often on top of the leader.

the fish for its mystery, strength, and desirability, but rarely will you see an authority trying to explain *why* it comes to the fly—only how to tie and present the flies.

By a quirk of the last ice age, we in North America do have landlocked Atlantic salmon in the pure, cold waters of the northeastern United States and eastern Canada. These fish are taxonomically identical to their sea-run brethren, although they don't grow as large. A 5-pound fish is a good catch.

While some rivers enjoy year-round populations of landlocks that can be as selective as trout, the best angling with a fly rod occurs early in the year as the fish leave their favored lakes to follow spawning feed fish up into rivers and streams. In the autumn they return to the rivers again, this time to make their own spawning runs. Their main and preferred forage is smelt, although they will take alewives and insects. They fight with the strength and stamina of their sea-run brethren, and their leaps can be astoundingly high.

There are five species of Pacific salmon: chinook, also known as king salmon; coho, known as silver salmon; pink; sockeye; and chum. While Atlantic salmon can and do make more than one run into and out of their natal rivers to spawn, Pacific salmon make only one spawning run and then die. As with Atlantics, a variety of man-made problems, such as dams, commercial overharvesting, and pollution, have reduced the once astounding runs of Pacific salmon. The problems have been identified, and national and international efforts are underway to at least halt the decline and hopefully reverse it. Only in northern Canada and Alaska have salmon numbers stayed strong, but there do remain fishable populations in Northern California, Washington, Oregon, and British Columbia.

Chinooks and cohos, along with steelheads, constitute a group of big, strong migrating fish that will take a fly, especially on their spawning runs up into West Coast rivers, and all fight tenaciously when hooked. Although none of these fish actively feed during their spawning runs, the reason they hit a fly seems less mysterious than with Atlantics. Big pulsing flies fished wet and deep on sinking lines are favored; when these are drifted in front of holding fish, a fish will sometimes strike out of apparent irritation.

Steelhead, cohos, and chinooks have been successfully introduced into the Great Lakes, which serve as freshwater oceans for the fish. Gorging on abundant alewives, the fish grow very large and provide great sport for trolling anglers.

Although their spawning success is minimal, these stocked fish do migrate up into the rivers and streams that drain into the Great Lakes, providing good opportunity

Landlocked salmon are taxonomically identical to Atlantic salmon. They do not, however, migrate to the sea, instead migrating out of lakes and up rivers to spawn. In addition, landlocked salmon are attuned to freshwater organisms, taking flies that imitate insects and forage fish, especially smelt.

Steelhead are sea-run rainbow trout. Like Atlantic salmon, they are referred to as *anadromous*, meaning they spend the majority of their lives feeding and growing in the ocean and then return to streams and rivers to spawn. They're mainly a West Coast fish but have been successfully introduced into large lakes across the continent, notably the Great Lakes, where they thrive.

for fly fishers. Because of their popularity, crowding on the more famous streams, such as the Salmon River in Pulaski, New York, can be a problem, but more and more anglers are finding good success on smaller, out-of-the-way streams, especially in late autumn and early spring.

OTHER FRESHWATER QUARRY

It might be wrong to say that every freshwater fish provides good opportunities for fly-rodders, but it wouldn't be *too* far wrong. Except for fish that stay in deep water and out of reach, all freshwater fish can be caught on flies. In addition, more and more anglers are turning to the fly rod not just because it's more sporting and fun (although it is), but because the lifelike qualities of artificial flies make fly fishing a more productive and efficient way to catch fish.

Several species of freshwater fish are particularly well suited to fly fishing, and these are led by black bass (the genus *Micropterus*). Both largemouth *(M. salmoides)* and smallmouth *(M. dolomieu)* bass are good fly fishing quarry, but for different reasons.

Largemouths live in relatively shallow, weedy water and around submerged vegetation. They are voracious predators of nearly anything they can swallow. Flies have been created to imitate frogs, salamanders, worms, and, of course, smaller feed fish. And while floating lines are usually perfect for hopping that deer hair frog or popper across the lily pads, sinking lines can put underwater flies at the exact depths, which rarely exceed 10 feet, where early- or late-season largemouths might be holding.

Smallmouths are even better. In their cold-water, hard-bottom lake hideouts, a skimming surface Muddler or Matuka streamer fly will easily imitate panicked or injured feed fish. And there are now superb flies that imitate crayfish realistically.

But it's in flowing water that fly fishing for smallmouths is particularly effective. Many of the same flies and presentations you've learned for trout can be used for smallies. They'll certainly take surface insects when available, as well as small feed fish and crayfish. Creeping a weighted crayfish imitation across a rocky bottom makes it nearly irresistible. Down-and-across presentations of wet flies or streamers are effective, too, and swimming a big black Woolly Bugger in front of a hungry smallmouth is sure to bring a strike.

Pickerel and northern pike have been on-again, off-again targets of fly fishers for years. Their sporting qualities, especially on a fly rod, are undeniable. Put a 20-pound pike on the end of a 7-weight outfit, and you'll see just how hard a pike can fight. The trouble is that the best pickerel and pike fishing coincides with the best trout fishing, in late spring and early summer. (If you need to refresh your memory on line weight, refer back to pages 6–7 and the table on page 8.)

Yet if you focus on the ambush spots where pike and pickerel hold, on the edges of surface weedbeds early in the season and along submerged cover later, you'll find that they take fluttered or erratically swimming streamers quite willingly. More and more anglers are finding that fly rods and pike in the great northern Canadian waters provide exciting and nearly nonstop action all summer. Also, when the largemouth bass are off their feed or have been highly pressured, you can target pickerel in the same holding areas with large, bright streamers fished slowly in good cover.

Given our ingrained vision of carp as bottom feeders, it might sound odd to list them here as targets for fly-rodders. Yet in Europe, carp are considered worthy gamefish that grow big, come to the fly well, and put up great fights. Here in the United States, carp are widespread and abundant in the shallow, fertile waters they prefer. Having experienced so little

Smallmouth bass are an exciting fish to target with fly fishing equipment. They come well to the fly, whether in flowing or still water, strike hard, and fight exceptionally well. In addition, they feed on much the same forage as trout, making your standard collection of artificial flies—especially big nymphs and streamers—effective in catching them.

fishing pressure in this country, they have not acquired the notable wariness attributed to them in Europe.

Our misconceptions about carp come from lumping them into the same category as catfish and suckers; that is, as bottom feeders of detritus and carrion. Although carp can and do root along muddy bottoms, they also like sandy shoals, feed readily at and just under the surface, and use eyesight as often as their exceptional senses of smell and taste. Anglers who have pursued them often liken them to bonefish (which, by the way, are also bottom feeders). And as with bonefish, you should spot and stalk carp with a slow, careful approach and then present a dry fly or slowly sinking nymph carefully out in front of them. Then hang on. A 20-pound carp is a handful of fish.

Panfish are ideally suited to fishing with flies. They're numerous. They attack flies easily. They're tasty. And they're found almost everywhere. The term *panfish* refers to any number of usually small, schooling fish, including bluegills, pumpkin-

Northern pike (shown here) and pickerel provide excellent sport for the fly fisher. They are voracious predators that rarely allow a well-presented streamer to pass by. And they can reach impressive sizes, with pike regularly topping 10 pounds, and pickerel, 4 pounds. *(Will Ryan)*

seeds, sunfish, crappies, white and yellow perch, and others. While the standard vision of fly-rodding for panfish involves small popping bugs gurgled in close to overhanging bushes or submerged brush piles, and this is certainly effective and loads of fun, small streamers and swimming nymphs can also be used.

Especially when white or yellow perch are feeding subsurface or when crappies are chasing threadfin shad, swimming a small streamer or dragonfly nymph at their depth with a sink-tip or full sinking line will bring plenty of action. And don't be shy about taking a mess of panfish home. They're so numerous that fisheries managers encourage this, and they make tasty table fare.

SALTWATER FLY FISHING

The fastest growing segment of fly fishing is angling in salt water. This phenomenon is powered both by rejuvenated stocks of inshore fish that are easy to find and exciting to catch and by new fly fishing tackle designed to handle the rigors of ocean fishing.

You can certainly use your standard 6-weight trout outfit in salt water, but you shouldn't. Twenty- and 30-pound striped bass often forage within an easy cast from shore, and a fish that size will burn up your trout reel, strip off all your line and backing, and probably break your rod. You'll never forget the encounter, however.

If you're unsure to what degree you'd like to get involved with fly fishing in salt water, hire a guide who can provide the right equipment and show you what the experience is all about. Guides have appropriate rods and flies, and they'll know where the fish are.

If you do find that you'd like to have your own equipment for saltwater fly fishing, get an 8- to 10-weight fast-action rod with a reel that matches and an appropriate disk drag system. The reel should have plenty of room for backing behind the fly line. And get two (or more) spools: one for floating line and one for sinking. (Some folks would add a sinking-tip line and a shooting-head line segment attached to a full sinking line.) Add appropriate, heavier leaders to cast up to 1- or 0-sized flies, and you have a basic rig. For bigger, offshore gamefish such as billfish or sharks, you'll need heavier equipment, up to 14-weight rods and reels, at proportionately higher prices.

Saltwater fly fishing can be roughly divided into three types of angling defined by the waters you frequent: inshore, offshore, and flats. There's some minor overlap, especially between inshore and flats fishing, but in general the fish you'll be targeting can be grouped according to which habitats they frequent.

Inshore fishing for striped bass, bluefish, bonito, and little tunny (false albacore) has fueled much of the current interest in ocean fly fishing. This heightened interest coincides with the resurgent populations of striped bass up and down the Atlantic seaboard all the way from Maine and Nova Scotia to Florida and into the Gulf of Mexico. On the West Coast, stripers were successfully introduced to San Francisco Bay in the late 1800s and now form substantial stocks from California to Washington and even up to Vancouver Island.

The East Coast striper stocks, severely depleted in the 1970s and early 1980s, are back with a vengeance, thanks in large measure to a federal bureaucracy to protect them from the overfishing that decimated their numbers to begin with. It looks like they're back to stay, which is not to say that they're always easy to find. It's a big ocean out there.

All inshore gamefish are food driven. They'll seek out and follow a variety of forage including herring, menhaden, alewives, silversides, eels, smelt, sea worms, squid, and crabs. Find concentrations of bait, and you'll usually find stripers or bluefish nearby. And you'll find bait concentrations in tidal rips, saltwater ponds, estuaries, crashing surf, along rocky shoals and breakwaters, and even in deeper onshore waters.

Any forage concentration will usually attract bluefish as well as stripers when they're in the area (like stripers, bluefish are migratory), but the feeding behaviors of

With resurgent numbers of striped bass now available to saltwater anglers, and with their migratory paths up and down the Atlantic coast (and to a lesser degree, the Pacific coast) keeping them inshore and readily available, stripers have become a favorite target of fly fishers. Young schoolies, as they're known, will run from 4 to 7 pounds and provide excellent sport, but bigger fish from 8 to 30 pounds and larger are always possible.

these two fish are dramatically different. Stripers have an irritating habit of concentrating on just one type of forage at a time. If they have become enamored of squid, no herring or silversides imitation will work. This means that you either must know which forage is being targeted on a particular day, or you must change flies regularly until you find the right imitation.

With bluefish, you need merely to get your fly, almost any fly, into the school of feed fish they're working. A quick and erratic retrieve will often make your fly stand out and will draw slashing strikes. With stripers, not only do you need to match the food item, but you need to match the swim speed of the food, too. Often when stripers are working a school of feed fish, a medium retrieve of a like-colored streamer will work. Sometimes, especially in surf, the retrieve needs to be as fast as you can make it.

Note: The long casts that you can and should make will mean plenty of extra line at your feet. In a boat, keep the deck around you clear of obstructions; while ashore, a stripping basket—either a commercially made one or a plastic dishpan—tied to your waist is almost essential.

Offshore fly fishing for billfish or sharks requires first finding them and then getting close enough to cast a fly. Two basic methods are used. The first involves creating a *chum line*—a soup of chopped baitfish ladled onto the sea behind the boat—that will attract your quarry and draw them close to the boat. The second is trolling a teaser rig, much as you would for any method of blue-water gamefishing, and then bringing it and the target fish within reach of your fly. This is hard, specialized fishing; all but the most devoted and fanatical fly fishers should hire a charter boat that specializes in offshore gamefish and allows fly fishing.

Flats fishing is a find-and-stalk type of angling, but it's very exciting. While some guides and boats stalk striped bass on the flats of estuaries and brackish ponds, most flats fishing is in tropical or subtropical waters where the flats are extensive and the targeted fish are usually bonefish and permit. This type of fly fishing has been popular for some time and has become more so with conservation efforts and an unwritten no-kill policy. The numbers of fish have risen as a result, making what was once a very expensive sport, because of travel and specialization, more accessible for all anglers.

In flats fishing you must hunt for the fish, which will be feeding on crabs, shrimp, sea worms, and small fish in water seldom more than a few feet deep. Having found the fish, you stalk them either by wading closer or poling a boat to within casting distance; then you put your fly far enough in front that it sinks to the bottom in front of the fish. As you might guess in these shallow, hazardous (for the fish) waters, stealth is your greatest ally. But the rewards are great, as these superbly strong fish sizzle line off a reel again and again before being landed.

Of note among the many fish that may be found in inshore waters as well as on the flats are red drum (known to most anglers as redfish) and tarpon. Redfish constitute a fine example of successful restoration efforts. Recently fished almost to the point of no return, redfish are now carefully protected and can be found in brackish estuaries and flats as well as in- and offshore waters from Maine to Florida and all along the Gulf of Mexico. For fly anglers, stalking them in grass beds, where they feed on crabs and shrimp, is a favored method, but they're often found in inshore waters feeding on abundant schools of menhaden, mullet, and pinfish.

Tarpon are exceptionally strong and flashy fighters. Although most weigh 40 to 50 pounds, many are caught every year that weigh up to 100 pounds, and some can exceed 150. That's a real handful on a fly rod, especially when the fish burns off yards of line and leaps as high as 10 feet out of the water. Because they eat a wide variety of crabs and feed fish in tropical and subtropical waters, a large streamer cast in front of a pod of tarpons often brings hard strikes. They're often found in flats and grassy backwaters or in bays and estuaries. Since the mid-1950s, the state of Florida has carefully protected this marvelous resource, and finding tarpon is not difficult, although a good guide can be a big help.

The saltwater fish I've highlighted here are the stars of the show, but many other saltwater species can provide hours of fishing enjoyment and don't necessarily require such specialized fly fishing gear. It's really a matter of finding out which fish swim in the sea close to you. In my opinion, casting to saltwater fish sure beats beach sand in a Speedo.

12 | Flies and Fly Tying

"Fly tying is the next best thing to fishing; it is the sort of licking of the lips that eases a thirsty man in the desert."

ARTHUR RANSOME
"FLY TYING IN WINTER," IN ROD & LINE, 1929

When all is said and done, after all the gear is explained, the techniques defined and learned, and the skills of fly fishing honed, you'll notice that our main focus and unending fascination is with the flies we tie onto our tippet. Everything else about fly fishing, perhaps with the exception of the fish themselves, is of secondary importance to selecting the right fly.

This is not a new or modern phenomenon. As long as eight hundred years ago, in the thirteenth century, German writers were describing "feathered hooks." Dame Berners listed a dozen patterns of flies from which to choose in her *Treatyse* in the year 1496. By 1676, Izaak Walton's list included sixty-five patterns. More recently, in 1950, J. Edson Leonard published a book, *Flies*, that included more than twenty-two hundred patterns. And these were all selective lists that omitted many other patterns and types.

In the last fifty years, with the rapid expansion of interest in fly fishing and the increase in the species of fish that are sought, has come a corresponding boom in hook technology and in the man-made materials that can be used to create novel and interesting artificial flies. The list of new patterns that has resulted is almost endless, and today there are thousands upon thousands of flies to choose from.

With so many patterns, classifying them into broad groups that reflect their most basic functions is a help. Just as we classify living organisms to better understand them (kingdom, phylum, class, order, family, genus, species), these broad groupings help us sort out the functions of artificial flies and make it easier to decide which flies to use when.

ATTRACTOR FLIES

Attractor flies don't imitate any specific insect or food item. Fish would certainly take exception to this statement, because when they take any fly, they're usually looking

Attractor flies *(clockwise from top left)*: Royal Coachman (dry fly), Royal Wulff (dry fly), Hornberg (streamer), Mickey Finn (streamer), Professor (wet fly). *(Orvis, Jim Dugan)*

for a meal. These flies, however, were invented and are still tied simply to attract the attention of a fish. Developed and refined through long use, they have proven exceptionally versatile and productive over the years.

Attractors draw attention through the use of colors, action, or both. The fly might be tied within one or more of the standard classifications: as a dry fly, wet fly, or streamer. The Royal Coachman and its variations, like the Royal Wulff or the Royal Trude, are classic examples of attractor dry flies—although the Royal Coachman was originally tied, and sometimes still is, as a wet fly. Old standard wet flies like the Professor or the Parmachene Belle are typical attractors, as are such streamers as the Mickey Finn and the Light and Dark Edson Tigers.

Attractors are often used when we have no idea what the fish are finding for food or, more commonly, in relatively infertile waters, when the fish are anxious to sample anything that might be food. Our primary goal in either case is to draw attention to the fly—thus the bright colors and sometimes erratic action.

The vast majority of Atlantic salmon flies are attractor flies, and thank goodness they work. Because Atlantic salmon fly innovators are limited only by their own imaginations and skills, some of the most intricate and beautiful examples of the fly tier's craft are represented by these beautiful concoctions. Of course, there are many workaday salmon flies, too, that any fly tier can put together. One of the highlights of my career as a fly tier and fisher came when I landed a big hen salmon on a tiny Undertaker wet fly that I had tied less than an hour before.

ALL-PURPOSE FLIES

All-purpose flies do not imitate specific *items* of food; rather, they imitate specific *types* of foods. All-purpose nymphs like a Hare's Ear, Whitlock's Red Squirrel, or Gartside Sparrow are chosen because we can be fairly certain the fish are feeding on nymphs, but we either don't know what the specific insect is or don't have an exact imitation.

Similarly, there are all-purpose dry flies, of which the Adams might be the most famous. Its generic gray body and mix of grizzly and brown hackle, along with its grizzly wings, make it a sort of everyday workaholic dry fly. Personally, I turn to an Adams whenever I'm not sure what the fish are rising to and sometimes even when I'm pretty sure I do. Adams dry flies just simply work.

Other notable all-purpose dries include most of the Wulff patterns. These are named for Lee Wulff, who decided that white hair wings and heavily dressed large flies were ideal for heavy, choppy water because you could see the fly more easily, and so could the fish. They don't imitate anything specifically, except food.

The fantastically productive Humpies are good all-purpose dry flies. Those deer hair shells and wings, along with the array of colorful floss bodies, stand out in a stream. Created in the West and tied originally as a beetle, the Humpy is highly productive in many of the heavy-flowing mountain streams there. I know an exceptional angler, Spence Conley, who swears by Humpies, particularly chartreuse-bodied Humpies, in nearly any water or situation. And Spence catches a lot of fish with them.

Even streamers include examples of extraordinary all-purpose flies. The Muddler

All-purpose flies *(clockwise from top)*: Hare's Ear (nymph), Muddler Minnow (streamer), Humpy (dry fly), Adams (dry fly). *(Jim Dugan)*

Minnow is just that—extraordinary. Originally tied to imitate a specific fat-head minnow, the Muddler in its many variations has proven versatile throughout the country and in a wide variety of situations.

This versatility is typical of many all-purpose flies. Often invented to imitate a specific organism, they have somehow acquired a universal quality that transcends the imitation and becomes broadly effective. The Adams is also like this; it was first tied to imitate a caddisfly.

IMITATOR FLIES

Imitator flies are tied to represent a specific food item. When we use a Blue-Winged Olive dry fly, the materials, construction, and size of the fly are chosen to imitate a specific mayfly dun. The same is true of many nymphs, streamers, and, in some cases, wet flies. The Hexagenia nymph imitates that great, slow-water mayfly nymph, the Gray Ghost imitates a smelt, and the Alder wet fly looks just like a swimming caddisfly.

Imitator flies have given us the greatest variety of patterns, mainly because of the huge variety of forage that fish will consume. If trout are finding tiny, cream-colored duns to their liking, they'll often feed on the duns exclusively or perhaps in conjunction with the corresponding nymph, both of which patterns we'll certainly want to carry.

In addition, there will always be times when we don't think the standard pattern is quite right for some reason. For instance, although the Hendrickson Dun is imitated with a light version, a dark version, and a quill-bodied version, sometimes none of them works. Perhaps the dubbing along the thorax ought to be thicker or a different color, an angler might think, or the hackle should be mottled instead of simply a dark dun color. In an hour, a new imitator fly might be invented.

Imitator fly names might not be as recognizable as some of the attractor or all-purpose patterns, but when they're designed to imitate a specific hatch or food item, they can be lumped into a class with other such imitations. For instance, there are dozens of patterns that imitate that prolific and long-lasting Western hatch of mayflies (order Ephemeroptera), the Pale Morning Dun (genus *Ephemerella*, species *inermis* and *infrequens*). I personally own two dozen versions of the Pale Morning Dun dry fly, some of them called just the Pale Morning Dun but others called by such descriptors as the Tiny Cripple PMD, the Half Back, and the PMD Comparadun. It's only important to me to know that they all are intended to imitate the *Ephemerella* mayflies.

Just as there are genera of mayflies (nearly thirty!), caddisflies, and stoneflies—which we then classify further into species, such as Hendricksons (*Ephemerella subvaria*), zebra caddis (*Macrostemum zebratum*), and salmon flies (*Pteronarcys californica*), re-

Imitator flies *(clockwise from top)*: Blue-Winged Olive (dry fly), Pale Morning Dun (dry fly), Dark Hendrickson (dry fly), Gray Ghost (streamer). *(Orvis)*

spectively—there are subclasses of dry flies, wet flies, nymphs, and streamers. Understanding these further breakdowns is always a help when selecting flies to buy or tie.

DRY FLIES

Dry flies are intended to float on the surface film of the water, the meniscus. They are tied on light wire hooks and with materials that are also light and often water resistant. The most recognizable dry flies are those that have a stiff feather mounted on edge (the hackle), which is wound around the hook shank near the eye, but some have hackle wound on top or along their entire lengths, some have no hackle, and others use something else for buoyancy.

Dry flies are most effective when fish are feeding on specific insects on the water surface, but they're used in nearly any situation primarily because the angler can see the rise of the fish and the take of the fly.

When anglers talk about dry flies, they usually refer to them in one of two ways and sometimes both: by what the flies are intended to imitate and by the construction of the fly. Both descriptions, plus the size of the hook, help us determine which fly will be most productive in a given situation, especially where fish are highly pressured by anglers. For instance, the fish might be focused on a Blue-Winged Olive Dun that is about a ¼-inch long. This is descriptive of both the natural insect and the corresponding class of dry fly, but a size 18 parachute tie might be more productive than a size 18 thorax tie. The terms *parachute* and *thorax*, along with the hook size, refer to the construction of the fly. When we talk about what dry flies are *intended to imitate*, we're usually talking about a specific insect or a stage in its development. When we say a *dun*, as in Blue-Winged Olive Dun, we're talking about an imitation of a mayfly after it has stepped out of its nymphal shuck and onto the water surface. *Dun* indicates both the phase of the mayfly and the type of dry fly. Likewise, when we say *spinners*, we're referring to adult mayflies that drop dead onto the water after breeding and also to a fly that imitates them. Ergo, after the Blue-Winged Olive has mated we'll want to use a spinner, or spent-wing, dry fly that looks like the natural—specifically, a size 18 brown spinner imitation.

When speaking of imitative dry flies we're usually referring to one of these several insects or insect phases: duns and spinners (which are exclusively mayflies), emergers, floating nymphs, cripples, other adult insects, and terrestrials. Each of these describes both a specific insect or phase and the corresponding dry fly. Caddisflies and stoneflies don't have duns and spinners, so they're usually referenced directly: an Elk-Winged Caddis or a Salmonfly dry fly, for example. And terrestrial references are usually directly descriptive, such as a Hopper (grasshopper), Red Ant, Inchworm, or Jassid—dry flies all. When referring to the construction of a dry fly, we'll usually add a term such as standard hackle, Catskill tie, parachute, spent-wing, hair-wing, no-hackle, Comparadun, CDC, or thorax (see page 179). Other descriptions are used less often, such as reverse-tied, upside-down, loop-winged, and so on.

All these terms refer to a method of tying or a specific material. Standard-hackle dry flies have the hackle wound around the shank near the eye. Catskill ties have stan-

Dry flies *(clockwise from top):* Elk-Winged Caddis, Ausable Wulff, Stimulator, Floating Inchworm. *(Orvis)*

dard hackling but sparse bodies and tails. A parachute dry fly has the hackle wound around the wing above the hook shank so that the fly can ride lower on the meniscus. Spent-wing dries are for spinners or other insects that float splay-winged on the water. A hair-wing fly uses calf tail or some other hair or synthetic fiber for wings instead of feathers. No-hackle dries derive their buoyancy from body or wing material and have no hackle. Comparaduns use elk or deer hair to imitate the wings of the natural, and because the hair is hollow, the flies float well without any hackle. CDC refers to *cul de canard*, an oily, fluffy feather from a duck's butt that floats well. A thorax tie has its hackle angled both behind and in front of the wing, which makes the fly sit lower on the water and produces a perfect profile in the meniscus.

These labels and descriptions are not exhaustive, and with the continuing development of fly tying methods and materials, I'm sure more and more dry flies will be developed. Inevitably, however, the names of the most productive and memorable dry flies refer to their intended imitation, their construction, or both.

WET FLIES

There are really only two types of wet flies: those that have wings made from stiff feathers such as duck quills or turkey wing feather segments and those that are wingless. In the former, the wings not only make the fly look like something alive—especially a diving caddisfly—but also help keep it "swimming" on an even keel and upright. Most winged wet flies also have some soft hackle tied under the eye to imitate legs and give more action to the fly.

These winged wet flies include *(left to right)* a Royal Coachman, a Professor, a Montreal, a Golden Pheasant, and a Scarlet Ibis.

There are many effective wingless wet flies. These simply have some long or short soft hackle wound around the hook shank and swept back along it so that the hackle pulsates when the fly moves underwater.

Most wet flies are tied on heavier wet fly or nymph hooks so that they'll get down under the surface, and most are intended to be moved by the current or the angler to give their materials extra animation.

NYMPHS

Most artificial nymphs are tied to imitate the underwater life stages, or nymphs, of mayflies and stoneflies. Some confusion ensues when imitations of other underwater life forms, such as caddisfly and midge larvae and pupae, are also called nymphs. Suffice it to say that any fly designed to imitate underwater insects can be called a nymph.

Nymphs are tied in several ways. Unweighted nymphs can be tied on heavy nymph hooks or on lighter dry fly hooks. Because they're unweighted, the heavier hook nymphs are intended to be fished in rather shallow water where they can drift along without frequently catching on the bottom. The dry fly versions are light enough to imitate hatching insects that either have not been able to escape their nymphal shucks near the surface or are struggling to do so. These nymphs are fished in or just below the meniscus.

In weighted nymphs some structural weight is added before the materials are applied to the hook. This material was traditionally lead wire, but more recently a tin al-

Nymphs *(clockwise from top)*: Bead-Head Pheasant Tail, Bead-Head Prince, Pheasant Tail, Deep Sparkle Pupa. *(Jim Dugan)*

loy wire has replaced toxic lead. These nymphs sink quickly and are meant to be fished on the bottom, where fish do the majority of their feeding.

Bead-head nymphs have brass, steel, or tungsten beads incorporated into the pattern, usually just behind the hook eye. The bead heads help the fly sink fast and add an attractor element to the pattern. The beads generally come in brass, copper, or silver colors, while some beads are now black or red. Other materials can form beads, too, such as colored plastic or glass, but most often these add only to the pattern, not the weight of the fly.

STREAMERS

Traditional streamer flies are tied on heavy hooks, usually with a long shank to imitate feed fish. The body material is applied as on most other flies, yet because the material covers the entire shank, a streamer has the long, sleek look of a shiner.

It's the application of the feathers at the eye of the hook that gives traditional streamers their lifelike quality. These feathers, usually four of them, are tied at the eye on top of the hook and sweep back above the shank to the bend or beyond. They are usually tied in pairs, with the dull sides of two feathers facing the dull sides of the opposing pair. The glossy sides of the feathers are visible to the fish. Sometimes other feathers are added to the side of the fly to imitate depth or eyes. Either moving the streamer or manipulating it through moving water gives the artificial life and attraction.

A few new and different streamer patterns have recently become popular and

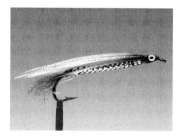

Streamers *(clockwise from top)*: Black-Nosed Dace, Joe's Smelt, Woolly Worm, Olive Woolly Bugger *(Jim Dugan, Orvis)*.

productive, especially the previously mentioned Muddler Minnow, hair-wing streamers like the Black-Nosed Dace, and the Thunder Creek streamers that use deer hair to form bullet-shaped heads and then sweep the hair back along the shank for motion. Other innovations include the addition of weighted eyes to hair-wing flies that are tied to swim with the hook point up or down, and a series of streamers coated with epoxy.

There's also a popular group of flies known as Woolly Worms or Woolly Buggers. Woolly Worms have fuzzy bodies that are wrapped with a hackle feather from back to front in a process known as *palmering*. At the eye of the hook more hackle is applied. The effect when the fly is fished underwater is that it looks like, well, a flailing woolly worm. Woolly Buggers are similar to Woolly Worms, but they have a tail extension of marabou feathers that absolutely comes to life when underwater. Either of these can be fished like a streamer or like a nymph, and they catch bunches of fish.

SALTWATER FLIES

Saltwater flies are usually tied on stainless steel hooks and can be huge. They incorporate a higher proportion of synthetic materials to help combat the destructive effects of big toothy fish and salt water. Most saltwater flies are streamer-like and need to be moved in the water or manipulated in tidal flows. Many patterns, however, are tied as surface swimmers or poppers that are used to attract attention.

Saltwater flies are very often chosen to match the food the gamefish are taking: bait like menhaden, squid, crabs, or sea worms. Some effective and lifelike flies are now being produced.

FLY TYING

This eternal fascination with artificial flies explains why many fly fishers turn to tying their own. There may be other, additional reasons, such as the need to match specific insects streamside, the inability to buy a preferred pattern or well-tied flies locally, or the perception that you can produce your own flies much more inexpensively than you can buy them. Whatever the reason, tying flies is a natural extension of the fly fishing experience.

The *craft* of fly tying is not difficult to learn if your initial motive is to tie basic flies that will catch fish. You need some rudimentary tools and materials to start with, but the basic method is essentially the same for almost any fly you tie. But the *art* of fly tying, like any art, is acquired only through years of experience, experimentation, and observation. Artistic flies can be complex blends of materials that are breathtaking to behold, like many of the classic full-dress Atlantic salmon flies, or extremely skilled tiers can concoct exacting imitations of insects that would fool the wariest of trout and the most discerning of human observers. Most of us tiers fall somewhere between, able to tie a variety of effective flies that catch fish in a number of situations.

The tools of the trade include a fly tying vise that will hold the hook. Try to get one that will hold a broad range of hooks of varying sizes. You'll need a bobbin that holds a spool of tying thread and has a tube attached through which the single strand of thread passes. The thread is what holds all the materials on the hook. You'll need some small, sharp, needle-nose scissors to clip materials. A dubbing needle or bodkin—a stout needle with a handle—will help. Hackle pliers hold the hackle that you'll wrap around the hook. Head cement, a liquid glue, adds to the durability of the fly. And you'll need hooks—dry fly, wet, and nymph hooks, streamer hooks, and stainless steel saltwater hooks. A pattern book—and there are hundreds of them—will help you know which materials are placed where to attain a desired effect.

While there are a few variations, almost all flies are tied from the bend in the hook toward the eye, and almost all are started by covering the hook shank with a full wrapping of tying thread to help prevent the materials from slipping around on the

The tools of the fly tier are unique because of the specialized techniques involved in tying flies. Fly tying is one of very few manufacturing operations that has never been mechanized. Each fly you see, use, or tie must be handmade. These tools are a vise (for holding the hook), a bobbin (for dispensing tying thread), dubbing needle, needle-nose scissors, and small and large hackle pliers. *(Cabela's)*

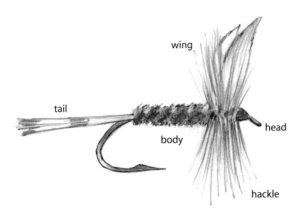

The basic parts of an artificial fly as represented by a Catskill-type dry fly.

smooth steel hook. Wind from the eye to the bend. At the bend, tie in the tail, often feather barbules but sometimes hair, quills, wool, or man-made fibers. Add a strand of tinsel or wire that will form the segments on the body when wrapped over it. The abdomen of the fly is usually some fine fur (dubbing) that's wound onto the tying thread with wax and then wrapped around the hook shank. Abdomens can also be created from tinsel, feather quills, herl, or a number of synthetic materials. The thorax of the fly is the thicker part of the body closer to the eye and is often just more dubbing wound on. Leave room between the thorax and the eye to complete the fly. This area often includes the wings of the fly and windings of hackle that will stand on edge to help the fly float or to give life to an underwater fly. With the tying thread, form a small head in front of the hackle and abutting the eye, tie it off, and apply head cement. You're done. (See the bibliography for reference works that go into much more detail about tying methods.)

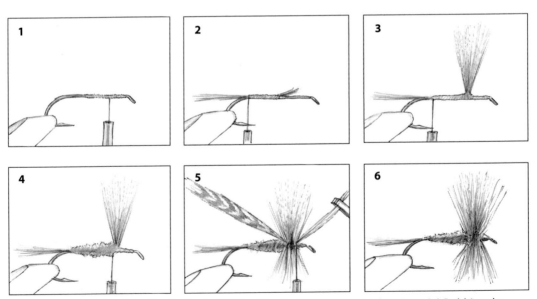

(1) Attaching the tying thread to the hook. **(2)** Attaching the tail. **(3)** Tying in the wings. **(4)** Dubbing the body. **(5)** Winding on the first hackle feather, with the second tied in and waiting to be wound. **(6)** After tying off the thread, the finished dry fly.

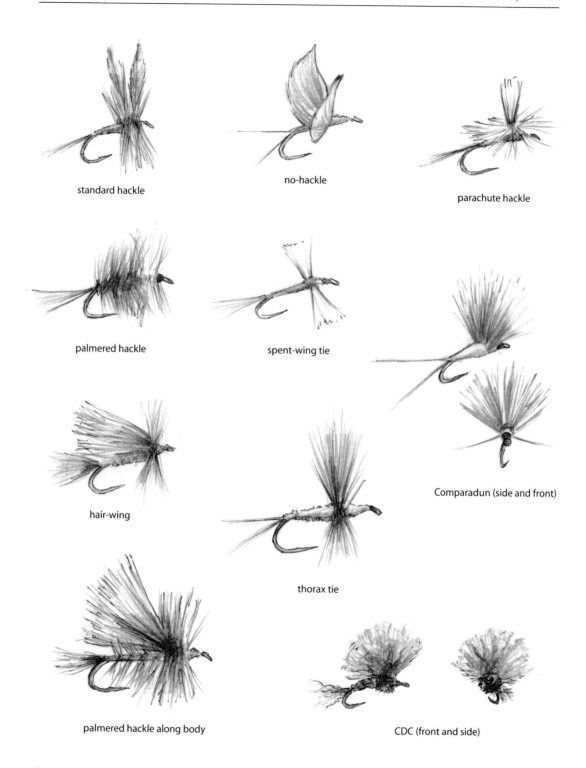

standard hackle

no-hackle

parachute hackle

palmered hackle

spent-wing tie

Comparadun (side and front)

hair-wing

thorax tie

palmered hackle along body

CDC (front and side)

Terms used in dry-fly construction.

Most pattern listings, and there are plenty of books that simply list flies and how to tie them, give their formulas in this order: hook type and size, thread size and color, then materials from the back of the fly at the bend to the front.

TOM'S TERRIFIC TWENTY-FOUR FOR TROUT

Whether you buy flies, acquire them from friends, or take up fly tying, you'll find unending fascination with their use, their materials and construction, and the abundance of thought and skill that have been invested in them. But you'll also need a guide to help you start your collection. Here's my core collection (see photos on inside covers):

ATTRACTOR FLIES: *dry*—Royal Wulff; *wet*—Parmachene Belle; *streamers*—Mickey Finn, Hornberg.

ALL-PURPOSE FLIES: *dry*—Adams, Ausable Wulff, Humpy (red); *wet*—Cahill, Brown Hackle; *nymphs*—Hare's Ear, Deep Sparkle Pupa; *streamers*—Muddler Minnow, Olive Woolly Bugger.

IMITATOR FLIES: *dry*—Hendrickson, Blue-Winged Olive Parachute, March Brown, Elk Hair Caddis, Stimulator; *wet*—Leisenring Black Gnat, Alder; *nymphs*—Pheasant Tail, Prince; *streamers*—Black-Nosed Dace, Joe's Smelt.

Bibliography

Ames, Thomas, Jr. *Hatch Guide for New England Streams*. Portland OR: Frank Amato, 2000.

Behnke, Robert J. *Trout and Salmon of North America*. New York: Free Press, 2002.

Caucci, Al, and Bob Nastasi. *Hatches II: A Complete Guide to Fishing the Hatches of North American Trout Streams*. New ed. Guilford CT: Lyons Press, 2004.

Flick, Art. *Art Flick's New Streamside Guide to Naturals and Their Imitation*. Guilford CT: Lyons Press, 1988.

Fuller, Tom. *The Complete Guide to Eastern Hatches: What Flies to Fish, When, and Where*. Woodstock VT: Countryman Press, 2004.

————. *Trout Streams of Southern New England: An Angler's Guide to the Watersheds of Massachusetts, Connecticut, and Rhode Island*. Woodstock VT: Countryman Press, 1999.

————. *Underwater Flies for Trout*. Woodstock VT: Countryman Press, 2003.

Hafele, Rick, and Dave Hughes. *The Complete Book of Western Hatches: An Angler's Entomology and Fly Pattern Field Guide*. Portland OR: Frank Amato, 1981.

Hughes, Dave, and Rick Hafele. *Western Mayfly Hatches: A Complete Guide*. Portland OR: Frank Amato, 2004.

Kaufmann, Randall. *Fly Patterns of Umpqua Feather Merchants: The World's 1,500 Best Flies*. 2nd. ed. Glide OR: Umpqua Feather Merchants, 1998.

Knopp, Malcolm, and Robert Cormier. *Mayflies: An Angler's Study of Trout Water Ephemeroptera*. Guilford CT: Lyons Press, 2002.

LaFontaine, Gary. *Caddisflies*. Rev. ed. New York: Lyons & Burford, [1996?].

Leeson, Ted, and Jim Schollmeyer. *The Fly Tier's Benchside Reference to Techniques and Dressing Styles*. Portland OR: Frank Amato, 1998.

Leonard, J. Edson. *Flies: Their Origin, Natural History, Tying, Hooks, Patterns and Selections of Dry and Wet Flies, Nymphs, Streamers, Salmon Flies for Fresh and Salt*. New York: Nick Lyons Books, 1988.

Marinaro, Vincent. *A Modern Dry-Fly Code*. New York: Lyons Press, 1997.

Meck, Charles R. *The Hatches Made Simple*. Woodstock VT: Countryman Press, 2002.

————. *Meeting and Fishing the Hatches*. Rev. ed. Lexington MA: Stephen Greene Press/Pelham Books, 1990.

————. *Trout Streams and Hatches of Pennsylvania: A Complete Fly-Fishing Guide to 140 Streams*. 3rd ed. Woodstock VT: Countryman Press, 1999.

Meck, Charles R., with Bryan C. Meck and D. Craig Josephson. *Mid-Atlantic Trout Streams and Their Hatches: Overlooked Angling in Pennsylvania, New York, and New Jersey*. Woodstock VT: Countryman Press, 1997.

Meck, Charles R., and Greg Hoover. *Great Rivers—Great Hatches*. Harrisburg PA: Stackpole, 1992.

Meck, Charles R., and John Rohmer. *Arizona Trout Streams and Their Hatches: Fly-Fishing in the High Deserts of Arizona and Western New Mexico*. Woodstock VT: Countryman Press, 1998.

Ryan, Will. *Northern Pike*. New York: Lyons Press, 2000.

————. *Smallmouth Strategies for the Fly Rod*. New York: Lyons & Burford, 1996.

Schollmeyer, Jim. *Hatch Guide for Lakes: Naturals and Their Imitations for Stillwater Trout Fishing*. Portland OR: Frank Amato, 1995.

————. *Hatch Guide for the Lower Deschutes River*. Portland OR: Frank Amato, 1994.

————. *Hatch Guide for Western Streams*. 3rd ed. Portland OR: Frank Amato, 2003.

Schullery, Paul. *American Fly Fishing: A History*. Rev. ed. New York: Lyons Press, 1999.

Schultz, Ken. *Ken Schultz's Fishing Encyclopedia: A Worldwide Angling Guide*. Foster City CA: IDG Books Worldwide, 2000.

Sosin, Mark, and Lefty Kreh. *Practical Fishing Knots II*. New York: Lyons & Burford, 1991.

Stewart, Dick, and Farrow Allen. *Flies for Trout*. North Conway NH: Mountain Pond, 1993.

Whitlock, Dave. *Dave Whitlock's Guide to Aquatic Trout Foods*. New York: Lyons & Burford, [1996?] c1982.

Resources

Here are a few organizations you might find helpful in your quest for greater fly fishing and conservation knowledge. Keep in mind there are hundreds, if not thousands, of local and regional groups around the country, so do some research in your neck of the woods to find the best match for you.

ORGANIZATIONS

Americans for Our Heritage and
    Recreation (AHR)
1615 M St. NW
Washington DC 20036
202-429-2666
Fax: 202-429-2621
E-mail: ahr@ahrinfo.org
www.ahrinfo.org
Americans for Our Heritage and Recreation (AHR) is a broad and diverse organization representing conservationists, the recreation and sporting goods industries, park and recreation specialists, wildlife enthusiasts, advocates for urban and wilderness areas, preservationists of cultural and historic sites, land trust advocates, the youth sports community, and civic groups seeking to revitalize the Land and Water Conservation Fund (LWCF) and the Urban Park and Recreation Recovery Program (UPARR).

Becoming an Outdoorswoman (BOW)
Diane Lueck / Christine Thomas
College of Natural Resources
University of Wisconsin—Stevens Point
800 Reserve St.
Stevens Point WI 54481
877-BOWOMAN (877-269-6626);
    715-228-2070
www.uwsp.edu/cnr/bow/
BOW offers outdoor skills workshops to women throughout North America.

The Conservation Fund
1800 North Kent St., Suite 1120
Arlington VA 22209-2156
703-525-6300
Fax: 703-525-4610
E-mail: postmaster@
    conservationfund.org
www.conservationfund.org
The Conservation Fund forges partnerships to preserve our nation's outdoor heritage—America's legacy of wildlife habitat, working landscapes, and community open-space.

Federation of Fly Fishers
P.O. Box 1595
Bozeman MT 59771-1595
406-585-7592
Fax: 406-585-7596
E-mail: conserve@fedflyfishers.org
www.fedflyfishers.org
The mission of the Federation of Fly Fishers is to lead activities that enhance and support the fly fishing experience for all anglers who fish with the artificial fly.

FishAmerica Foundation
225 Reinekers Lane, Suite 420
Alexandria VA 22314
703-519-9691
Fax: 703-519-1872
E-mail: info@asafishing.org
www.fishamerica.org/content/conservation/fishamerica/
FishAmerica's mission is to provide funding, without preference to species or geographic location, for hands-on projects at the local level. These projects enhance fish populations, water quality, and/or applied fisheries research in North America—thereby increasing the opportunity for sportfishing success.

Fish Unlimited
P.O. Box 1073
Shelter Island Heights NY 11965
631-749-3474
Fax: 631-749-3476
E-mail: fish@fishunlimited.org
www.fishunlimited.org
Fish Unlimited was created as a national clean water/fisheries conservation membership organization. Now, with over 8,400 members, they are dedicated to eliminating water pollutants and to returning the stocks of finfish and shellfish to their optimum health.

International Women Fly Fishers (IWFF)
141 Wiggins Court
Pleasant Hill CA 94523
925-934-2461
E-mail: pemagnuson@attbi.com
www.intlwomenflyfishers.org
IWFF is a nonprofit international women's organization formed to promote and educate women in the sport of fly fishing.

Izaak Walton League
707 Conservation Lane
Gaithersburg MD 20878
800-IKE-LINE (800-453-5463);
   301-548-0150
Fax: 301-548-0146
E-mail: general@iwla.org
www.iwla.org
One of the oldest conservation organizations in the U.S.

Land Trust Alliance (LTA)
1331 H St. NW, Suite 400
Washington DC 20005-4734
202-638-4725

Fax: 202-638-4730
E-mail: lta@lta.org
www.lta.org
The Land Trust Alliance (LTA) has helped build a strong land trust movement in America that now includes more than 1,260 conservation organizations.

National Fish and Wildlife Foundation
1120 Connecticut Ave. NW, Suite 900
Washington DC 20036
202-857-0166
Fax: 202-857-0162
www.nfwf.org
The National Fish and Wildlife Foundation conserves healthy populations of fish, wildlife, and plants, on land and in the sea, through creative and respectful partnerships, sustainable solutions, and better education.

The Nature Conservancy
4245 North Fairfax Dr., Suite 100
Arlington VA 22203-1606
800-628-6860; 703-841-5300
E-mail: comment@tnc.org
http://nature.org/
The Nature Conservancy's mission is to preserve the plants, animals, and natural communities that represent the diversity of life on Earth by protecting the lands and waters they need to survive.

Sierra Club
85 Second St., 2nd Floor
San Francisco CA 94105

415-977-5500
Fax: 415-977-5799
E-mail: information@sierraclub.org
www.sierraclub.org
The Sierra Club is America's oldest, largest, and most influential grassroots environmental organization.

Theodore Gordon Flyfishers (TGF)
P.O. Box 2345
Grand Central Station
New York NY 10163
E-mail: president@tgf.org
www.tgf.org
Founded 41 years ago by Ernest Schwiebert, Lee Wulff, Ed Zern, and other legendary anglers, Theodore Gordon Flyfishers (TGF) is a not-for-profit organization dedicated to promoting catch-and-release fly fishing, and to preserving and enhancing the coldwater fisheries that sustain our sport.

Theodore Roosevelt Conservation Partnership (TRCP)
555 Eleventh St. NW, 6th Floor
Washington DC 20004
202-508-3449
E-mail: comments@trcp.org
www.trcp.org
The TRCP is a nonprofit organization with a national focus on issues affecting hunting and angling powered by a nationwide foundation of 80,000 individual hunters and anglers and over 1,200 Affiliate clubs and organizations. The vision of the TRCP is

nothing less than a return of conservation to the top tier of America's national priorities. The TRCP will play a significant role in organizing America's millions of unaffiliated hunters and anglers to make their voice heard in Congress and in America's statehouses to reestablish conservation as a national priority.

Trout Unlimited
1500 Wilson Blvd., #310
Arlington VA 22209-2404
800-834-2419
Fax: 703-284-9400
E-mail: trout@tu.org
www.tu.org
Trout Unlimited's mission is to conserve, protect, and restore North America's trout and salmon fisheries and their watersheds.

Trust for Public Land (TPL)
116 New Montgomery St., 4th Floor
San Francisco CA 94105
415-495-4014
Fax: 415-495-4103
E-mail: info@tpl.org
www.tpl.org
The only national nonprofit working exclusively to protect land for human enjoyment and well-being.

GOVERNMENT AGENCIES

Bureau of Land Management (BLM)
Office of Public Affairs
1849 C St. NW
Washington DC 20240
202-452-5125
Fax: 202-452-5124
www.blm.gov
The Bureau of Land Management (BLM), an agency within the U.S. Department of the Interior, administers 261 million surface acres of America's public lands, located primarily in 12 Western States. The BLM sustains the health, diversity, and productivity of the public lands for the use and enjoyment of present and future generations.

Land and Water Conservation Fund (LWCF)
USDA Forest Service
P.O. Box 96090
Washington DC 20090-6090
202-205-1359
E-mail: dmccaig/r3_santafe@fs.fed.us
www.fs.fed.us/land/staff/LWCF/
The Land and Water Conservation Fund (LWCF) was established by Congress in 1965. The Act designated that a portion of receipts from offshore oil and gas leases be placed into a fund annually for state and local conservation, as well as for the protection of our national treasures (parks, forest, and wildlife areas).

U.S. Fish and Wildlife Service
Department of the Interior
1949 C St. NW
Washington DC 20240
800-344-WILD (800-344-9453);
    703-358-1718
E-mail: contact@fws.gov
www.fws.gov
*The U.S. Fish and Wildlife Service works
    with others to conserve, protect, and en-
    hance fish, wildlife, and plants and
    their habitats for the continuing benefit
    of the American people.*

USDA Forest Service
1400 Independence Ave. SW
Washington DC 20250-0002
202-205-8333
E-mail: webmaster@fs.fed.us
www.fs.fed.us
*The Forest Service manages public lands in
    national forests and grasslands.*

Index